By Spellbook & Candle

Cursing, Hexing, Bottling & Binding

By Spellbook & Candle

Cursing, Hexing, Bottling & Binding

Compiled by

Mélusine Draco

Winchester, UK
Washington, USA

First published by Moon Books, 2012
Moon Books is an imprint of John Hunt Publishing Ltd., Laurel House, Station Approach,
Alresford, Hants, SO24 9JH, UK
office1@jhpbooks.net
www.johnhuntpublishing.com
www.moon-books.net

For distributor details and how to order please visit the 'Ordering' section on our website.

Text copyright: Mélusine Draco 2011

ISBN: 978 1 78099 563 2

A CIP catalogue record for this book is available from the British Library.

Design: Stuart Davies

Printed and bound by CPI Group (UK) Ltd, Croydon, CR0 4YY

We operate a distinctive and ethical publishing philosophy in all
areas of our business, from our global network of authors to
production and worldwide distribution.

CONTENTS

Author Biography

Mélusine Draco is a magical instructor and author of numerous books on witchcraft and magic. Her *Traditional Witchcraft* series and *The Dictionary of Mystery & Magic* are published by Moon Books.

Setting the Scene

Curses have given the world its greatest stories, and the more grisly and gory, the better we like them. But cursing, or ill-wishing, is not confined to magical practitioners – black, white or grey – it is a form of expression intended to do harm in reparation for some real or imagined insult. And can be 'thrown' by anyone of any race, culture or creed without any prior experience of ritual magic or witchcraft.

Curses have also been taken seriously in literature. In *Phases in the Religion of Ancient Rome*, we discover that Roman poets Ovid and Horace recorded all manner of cursing in their writings. Or the most famous (albeit apocryphal) – that of the last Grand Master of the Knights Templar, which inspired six dramatic novels by French author Maurice Druon – *The Accursed Kings*.

Precious jewels connected to royalty and infamy have also inspired a variety of curses, especially where tragedy has repeatedly struck. As a result, the gems have been deemed to be cursed – with ruin and even death the unhappy lot of whoever owns them, as demonstrated in Simon Raven's contemporary novel, *The Roses of Picardie*.

Folklore also casts long shadows, with some infamy bringing a curse down on a family, which in turn has resulted in numerous tall tales, like Sir Arthur Conan Doyle's *The Hound of the Baskervilles*, featuring fictional detective Sherlock Holmes. Elizabethan curses appear in Shakespeare ... and the Bible, where the most vigorous and far-reaching are to be found in the Old Testament ... and in children's stories such as *Sleeping Beauty* and *Beauty and the Beast*. And how many schoolgirls have giggled over Tennyson's immortal lines: *'The curse has come upon me,'* cried the Lady of Shallot?

Confusingly, some curses have passed into the language – the 'Curse of Scotland' for example can refer to (1) the nine of diamonds in the game of Pope Joan – the Pope, the Antichrist of the Scottish reformers. (2) A great winning card in *comette*, introduced by Mary, Queen of Scots, and the curse of Scotland because it was the ruin of so many families. (3) The card on which the 'Butcher Duke' wrote his cruel order after the Battle of Culloden. (4) Or the arms of Dalrymple, Earl of Stair, responsible for the massacre of Glencoe. (5) The nine of diamonds is said to imply royalty and 'every ninth king of Scotland has been observed for many ages to be a tyrant and a curse to the country'. [*Tour Thro' Scotland*, Grose 1789]

The dictionary definition is: *To invoke or wish evil upon; to afflict; to damn; to excommunicate; evil invoked on another person,* but under what circumstances can we challenge this established way of thinking and ask ourselves: **Can cursing *ever* be justified?** And if we hesitate for just a moment, then we must ask the next question: *Is cursing evil?* The Christian priesthood obviously felt *their* cause was just and as a result, the Church's curses are so virulent that it's not just the 'victim' that suffers but their off-spring in successive generations. And if a curse is thrown at the perpetrator of some terrible crime, can it really be deemed to be evil?

One curse still heard quite regularly is: 'A plague on both their houses!' taken from Shakespeare's *Romeo and Juliet*. As John Wain observes in *The Living World of Shakespeare*, there is no reason, other than sheer stupidity and bloody-mindedness, that keeps the Montagues and Capulets at each other's throats. The blame for the subsequent tragedy is equally divided between both families and therefore the curse should strike both in equal retri-bution, so is considered justified.

Nevertheless, curses, like chickens, have a habit of coming home to roost. This is because if not properly 'earthed', curses return to the curser, just as chickens that stray during the day return to their roost at night.

Preparing the Way

A witch's ability to curse was exploited to the full by Church and Inquisition alike. 'Cursers are murderers,' wrote Richard Kilby in *The Burthen of a Loaden Conscience* [1616], 'for if it please God to suffer their curse to take effect, the party cursed is murdered by the Devil.' Although it was not invariably suspected that diabolical aid had been put to such use, many of those hauled up before the authorities to answer accusations of 'cursing' were ordinary *Christian* men and women.

A reputation for 'successful cursing' could easily lead to a formal charge of witchcraft, as in the case of 14-year-old Mary Glover. In 1602 the maid reported that one Elizabeth Jackson, having been turned away from the door, had wished 'an evil death to light upon her'. The girl died and at the trial much was made of Jackson's threats – 'the notable property of a witch'. Another instance of successful cursing was that of old Cherrie of Thrapston in Northamptonshire, who died in gaol in 1646 while awaiting trial as a witch. He had wished that his neighbour's tongue might rot off … and it did!

According to *Religion and the Decline of Magic*, this was to become the stock pattern of witchcraft accusations: *'When a bad-tongued woman shall curse a party, and death shall shortly follow, this is a shrewd token that she is a witch.'* Author Keith Thomas observes that it was ironic such presumptions should have been made so readily, in that if the curser had been provoked, it is hard to understand why contemporaries should have been so reluctant to see the outcome as *divine* judgement. 'The notion that God might avenge the poor by responding to their supplications was one which the Church, like society as a whole, seems to have been unwilling to face …' or cursing being seen as a means by which the defenceless tried to avenge themselves upon their enemies when the normal channels of legal action had been denied them.

Thomas warns it would be wrong to suggest all persons accused of witchcraft had malevolent thoughts about their neighbours, but it was the witch's 'traditional malignity' that rendered the charges plausible within the community. That was why some of the most powerful minds of the 17th century believed in punishing so-called witches, even though sceptical as to their actual powers. In other words, even if the accused *wasn't capable* of directing a successful curse, the mere token of the action itself was a declaration of malice towards another, and the witchcraft statues could be justified as a method of repressing malevolent feelings. But as one contemporary historian observed: *'If mere ill-will was to be punished then men would be driven to the slaughter-house in thousands.'*

Because of the low social station of many of those accused, modern researchers are also loath to believe witches of the time could exploit the psychological effects of a carefully placed curse. That said, cases recorded by anthropologists are of those of the Australian Aboriginal people, who do *not* have a formal training in psychology either! Neither do the Azande of Africa, who had been used as academic references for witchcraft for years.

Curses have been 'thrown' for the protection of homes, treasures, tombs and grave sites … the latter often remaining active for years. There are also records of curses being laid upon families, which have plagued them for generations – the Templar's curse reaching down through the ages to the death of Louis XVI on the guillotine. These were instruments of revenge or protection, and not placed by practitioners of witchcraft.

The longest Christian curse is the one placed by God on Adam and Eve when they were expelled from the Garden of Eden. While the solemn ritual of cursing that dates from the Middle Ages is excommunication; the *Catholic Encyclopaedia* describes the outcast as being *'considered as an exile from Christian society and as non-existent … in the sight of ecclesiastical authority'*.

The Church basing its right to curse on Mathew 18.18 where Jesus tells his disciples that *'whatever you bind on earth shall be bound in heaven'*.

The Old Testament's 'catalogue of maledictions' were so drastic that the Jewish congregations were frightened of hearing them read, in case they brought the curses down upon the listeners. These curses of *Hebrew* origin were the predecessors of the Christian rite of excommunication, more popularly known as 'Bell, Book and Candle'. Here the officiating cleric closes the book from which he has read the curse, a bell is tolled as for a dead man, and candles are extinguished as a sign that the soul of the offender has been moved from the sight of God. Even in the original version of the Church of England's *Book of Common Prayer* there is a relic from earlier times, a service called a *commination*, or 'denouncing of God's anger and judgement against sinners', which recalled some of the curses from the Old Testament. The medieval church laid this heavy imprecation on the heads of its excommunicated sinners:

> *Let him be damned in his going out and coming in.*
> *The Lord strike him with madness and blindness.*
> *May the heavens empty upon him thunderbolts*
> *and the wrath of the Omnipotent burn itself unto*
> *him in the present and future world. May the*
> *Universe light against him and the earth open*
> *to swallow him up.*
> [Pope Clement VI 1478-1534]

Perhaps one of the most well-known of ancient curses is that connected to the Egyptian boy-king, Tutankhamun, and placed at the time of his burial by the priesthood to protect the tomb of the young Pharaoh:

> *May death come on swift wings to him who*

disturbs the rest of the Pharaoh.

The world's press faithfully recorded the 'untimely' deaths of several members of the archaeological team involved in the 1922 excavation and the legend of the 'Curse' was firmly established as fact.

Nearer to our own times, the cursing well at Llanelian-yn-Rhos, near Colwyn Bay in Wales, was still doing a flourishing trade in the mid 19th century, and even the epitaph chosen by William Shakespeare for his own tomb was couched in the form of a curse:

Good friend, for Jesu's sake forbear
To dig the dust enclosed here.
Blest be the man that spares these stones
And curst be he that moves my bones.

In the esoteric encyclopaedia, *Man, Myth & Magic*, a curse is defined as the 'product of inner tension … even though few of us any longer expect the curse to do physical damage to its victims'. And while the author of *The Encyclopaedia of Witches & Witchcraft*, Rosemary Ellen Guiley, maintains that 'contemporary witchcraft does not condone cursing', the often-quoted piece by the late Evan John Jones, states quite categorically that one of the signs of a genuine witch is one who *does* have 'the power to call, heal and curse'.

So, let us make no bones about it, cursing, or ill-wishing *isn't* confined to witches, but when dealing with magic it is always advisable to have one or two tricks up our sleeves, as other folk may not be so reticent about demonstrating their magical prowess. We should also bear in mind a 'price' often exacted on those laying a curse, because if it should 'misfire', it will inevitably rebound on the sender. Think things through beforehand and do not fling a curse if a bottling or binding will do the trick.

This has nothing to do with the belief in the 'Three-Fold Return' – *all* magic must be 'earthed' in order for it to work, and if a spell hasn't been correctly directed, it *will* return to the sender just like a boomerang – because it has nowhere else to go!

This WARNING must be borne in mind by any potential curser. No matter what the books may tell you about spells for lifting curses ... *there is no such thing.* **Once sent, a curse cannot be lifted, called back, withdrawn or negated. It can, however, be deflected and,** *if the cause is not just,* **can be rebounded on the sender, especially if another magical practitioner is involved.**

Cursing & Hexing

Today a 'hex' refers to a curse intended to injure a person or his property: it's one of those words that has been misused for so long that it has practically changed its meaning. 'To hex' simply means to cast spells or 'practice witchcraft', although it's a relatively modern word in the English language, having come from a combination of Dutch and German ... the word *hexen*, meaning 'to practice sorcery'. The word is sometimes used synonymously with 'curse' although among some groups, 'hex' is used for both positive and negative spell casting. According to *The Encyclopedia of Witches & Witchcraft*, some modern witches use the term 'to hex' to describe a binding spell, which has an entirely different outcome from a curse.

In *Mastering Witchcraft*, Paul Huson reiterates that 'the art of magical warfare is not one to be undertaken lightly' and proceeds to catalogue a grisly collection of curses and counter-curses under the heading of 'Vengeance and Attack'. To set a curse requires a tremendous amount of time, effort and focus and, as Huson explains, in order to make your curse into something more than an empty threat, a witch needs to build a dark current or vortex of power. 'You are going to have to contact the abyss within you, and dredge up all those repressed hostilities and dark hatreds you have banished to the cellars of your mind from childhood onwards.'

Obviously it takes a long time to lay a successful curse and often may take several days before the witch has raised this dark energy by stoking up tightly controlled emotions in order to make the magic work. This is why a curse placed by a dying person can be so potent: every essence of their being is channelled into that last, final throw, which is intended to reach out from beyond the grave.

Curses come in all manner of forms, from the old Scottish

gibe: *'May you live in interesting times!'* to a full-blown ceremonial version (i.e. the Egyptian Curse) that can take days, or even a month, to prepare. Others can be found in all kinds of writing and if these words convey the essence of the curse you wish to send, then by all means use them. The poem *The Poison Tree* by William Blake is perfect for vengeance that goes back years; the nature and outcome of the curse will, of course, be influenced by the offence.

The Poison Tree

I was angry with my friend
I told my wrath, my wrath did end.
I was angry with my foe;
I told it not, my wrath did grow.

And I water'd it in fears,
Night & morning with my tears;
And I sunned it with smiles,
And with soft deceitful wiles.

And it grew both day and night,
Till it bore an apple bright;
And my foe beheld it shine,
And he knew that it was mine,

And into my garden stole
When the night had veil'd the pole.
In the morning glad I see
My foe outstretch'd beneath the tree.

The symbolic 'apple' used as a lure, should be one of the native crab varieties, but few folk would be persuaded to eat one if they were offered, never mind get it into their mind to steal one! It's a question of using 'soft deceitful wiles' and while mixing your own sugar concoction, visualise the face of your victim and imagine wasps becoming entrapped by sugar water in a jar, as you recite the poem. Better still if you have a photograph, sample of handwriting, or personal items belonging to the object of your spell place these, together with the slices of crab-apple and the sugar water into a jar – leave it outside and wait for the insects to arrive!

This second Blake poem, *The Sick Rose*, can also be used as a very potent charm ... again the strength of the curse will be influenced by the offence.

The Sick Rose

O Rose, thou art sick.
The invisible worm,
That flies the night
In the howling storm,

Has found out thy bed
Of crimson joy;
And his dark secret love
Does the life destroy.

As with all magical working, the charm should be repetitive, and spoken in such a way that the words reverberate in the witch's head throughout the casting. *The Sick Rose* is effective, simply because it is short and to the point. Take the bloom of a large, red rose and chop it into tiny pieces, mixing the broken petals with a shredded photograph and/or sample of handwriting, or any personal items (hair, nail clippings, etc.,) belonging to the object of your spell. Scatter the petals on the path or driveway of the offender's home, preferably at *'night in the howling storm'*.

As we can see from these two examples, any ordinary poem can be utilised to power a curse if the sentiments expressed by the poet echo those of the sender. The key is not necessarily *what* is said but the manner in *how* it is said, that brings about results. A curse thrown in a fit of rage or jealous pique might be extremely effective, but a knee jerk reaction might also rebound on the sender if the proper procedures aren't in place!

1. The Biblical Curse

Cursing can be found in most, if not all, religious traditions around the world. Although the content of these curses may vary, the purpose seems to be remarkably consistent: enforcement of law, assertion of doctrinal orthodoxy, assurance of community stability, harassment of enemies, moral teaching, protection of sacred places or objects, and so forth.

In the Bible, three different Hebrew words are translated as 'curse'. The most common is a ritualistic formulation, which described as 'cursed' those who violate community standards defined by God and tradition. Slightly less common is a word used to invoke evil against anyone who violates a contract or oath. Finally there are curses that are invoked simply to wish someone ill, like cursing a neighbour in an argument.

In general, the same people with the authority to bless also have the authority to curse. Within a Christian context a blessing is a pronouncement of good fortune on those initiated into God's plans, a curse is a pronouncement of ill fortune because of opposition to God's plans. The Christian or Jewish God may curse a person or a whole nation because of their opposition to His will; a priest may curse someone for violating God's laws. A curse is a deed requiring an authoritative figure performing the deed, and acceptance of this authority by those hearing it. Generally speaking, however, curses are usually placed by those *without* significant social power, or who singly lack power over those they wish to curse (such as a stronger enemy).

Conversely, although the precise term isn't generally used in this context, the concept of cursing plays a central role in Christian/Jewish theology. According to tradition, Adam and Eve are cursed by God for their disobedience; therefore, *all* of humanity is cursed with Original Sin. Jesus, in turn, takes this curse upon himself in order to redeem believers. [*Encyclopaedia Britannica*]

2. The Blacksmith's Curse (Ireland)

Because a blacksmith's anvil is a very ancient tool it has acquired symbolic meaning beyond its utilitarian use. *A Dictionary of Irish Mythology* by Peter Berresford Ellis, shows blacksmiths were credited with supernatural powers, echoing the old British Craft tradition of the magical ability of the smith. 'If a blacksmith, for nine consecutive mornings, rises before dawn, goes naked to the forge, turns the anvil nine times striking it three times after each turn, then no earthly power can neutralise any curse of his.'

A similar curse required the smith to turn the 'horn' of the anvil in the direction of the person being cursed, and to strike the anvil repeatedly, day and night, until the curse 'went home'.

3. The Blacksmith's Curse (English)

Refers to the tale in English folklore that the death of King William II – William Rufus, Norman King of England – was due to a curse thrown at his father, William the Conqueror, by a local blacksmith for taking the New Forest away from the common people.

> *But if you steal the land of an Englishman*
> *Then you will know this curse.*
> *Your first-born son's blood will run*
> *Upon the English earth.*
> **Part of the lyric of a contemporary ballad by English singer-songwriter, Frank Turner**

4. To Break Up a Couple (Voodoo)

If you don't have a valid reason for breaking up a couple's

relationship ... DON'T DO IT! This work should be performed during the waning moon and during the planetary hour of Mars. You will need:

A personal item from each person
1 lemon
Mars oil for anointing
Mars powder
Mars incense
Cayenne pepper or red pepper flakes
9 needles with the eyes broken
1 yard of black fabric
1 roll of cotton twine
An incense burner
Charcoal discs
9 black candles
Brown paper
Black ink and a pen
Red ink and a pen
6 aspirin tablets
Consecrated or holy water
A piece of steel wool
An empty, clean glass jar
1 bottle of Four Thieves Vinegar

Anoint the candles with oil and then coat with the pepper. Cut two squares of brown paper slightly larger than the diameter of the lemon. Write the names of both individuals nine times on their own piece of brown paper. Use black ink for the one you want to go away and red ink for the one you want to stay with you. When you are finished, carefully tear the edges of the paper so the edges are rough sided.

Beginning at the hour of Mars, light one candle, ignite the charcoal and burn one teaspoon of Mars incense. Cut the lemon in half and against one cut surface, press the personal item of the person it will represent into the flesh of the fruit. Sprinkle with holy water and say: *'I baptise you as [Name] in the name of the Father, Son and Holy Ghost.'*

Repeat the process with the other half of the lemon, targeting the second person in the relationship. Be careful not to mix them up. Now pick up the first half of the lemon and insert three aspirin into the flesh. As you do, say: *'[Name] your relationship with [Name] will sour. Every time you are in his/her presence a sour taste will come into your mouth.'*

Repeat this process with the second half of the lemon. This time state: *'[Name] your relationship with [Name] will sour. Every time you are in her/his presence a sour taste will come into your mouth.'*

Take both name papers and put an 'X' across the name, using your thumb. Make a statement of your intensions ... for example: *'I Cross you with the Spirits of Confusion and Strife, so that every time you are together, nothing but confusion and strife will result.'*

Sprinkle the 'X' on both papers with the pepper and make a statement on your intensions each time you apply a new ingredient. Ultimately each name will be crossed with oil, powder and pepper. Take each paper and place it on the respective half of the lemon, making sure the name is facing upwards. Put the two halves back together with a small piece of steel wool between them.

Begin to insert the nine needles around the lemon to hold the two halves together. As you insert the needles, curse the couple nine times – once completed, wrap the lemon in the black cloth and begin binding with the cotton twine. As you wrap the lemon, tie the twine in nine knots. Leave enough twine to form a loop for hanging the lemon. Once wrapped, suspend the lemon over the candle but not close enough for the flame to burn the cloth. For the next eight days, smoke the lemon in incense and then suspend it over the candle, repeating the curse; each night place the remaining candle wax and ash in a jar.

After nine days, cut off the twine and fabric from the lemon. Remove the nine needles and separate the lemon. Remove the name paper and lemon half of the person you desire and bury it in your garden in a place where the sun does not shine – i.e. under the house or a bush.

Place the lemon half and name paper of the one you want to leave in the glass jar with the nine needles, steel wool and all the candle wax and ashes from incense. Fill the jar with Four Thieves Vinegar. Wrap the jar in the black fabric and once again tie it up with twine, making nine knots as before. Go to a moving water source like a river, canal or stream and throw the jar over your left shoulder. Call the person by name and command them to leave. Walk away and don't look back.

Important: It is important that after each working that you take a cleansing bath and perform a ritual cleansing of the room in which you work. Most voodoo workings are long-term and involve a complex series of observances. Also bear in mind that voodoo usually combines the calling of old African tribal gods and Christian saints.

5. To Cause the Destruction of an Enemy (Satanic)

In the area of the altar produce the image of your victim, and proceed to inflict the destruction upon the effigy in the manner of your choice.

'This can be done in the following ways:

- The sticking of pins or nails into a doll representing your victim; the doll may be cloth, wax, wood, vegetable, etc.
- The creation of graphic imagery depicting the method of your victim's destruction; drawings, paintings, etc.
- The creation of a vivid literary description of your victim's ultimate end.

- A detailed soliloquy directed at the intended victim, describing his torments and annihilation.
- Mutilation, injury, infliction of pain or illness by proxy using any other means or devices desired.

Intense, calculated hated and disdain should accompany this step of the ceremony, and no attempt should be made to stop this until the expended energy results in a state of relative exhaustion on the part of the magician.'

[*The Satanic Bible*, Anton LaVey]

A Satanic rite require a great deal of pomp an ceremonial if it is going to succeed, and including a demon's name gives added impetus.

6. Christian Cursing

In most Christian-inspired writings we are led to believe that curses are the province of the witch but there is plenty of evidence that the Church acknowledges the reality of cursing by a fellow Christian. In *Proverbs* (26.2b) the Bible records that *'an undeserved curse does not come to rest'*, which can be understood as meaning that if you believe in the Christian God, then nothing can get at you. 'You do not need to worry about anyone casting any sort of pagan spell on you. Voodoo, witchcraft, hexes and curses have no power over you because you have been freed to worship God ...' explains an internet source.

Dennis Cramer, author of *Breaking Christian Curses*, has a very different viewpoint and suggests that other Christians *can* be responsible for ongoing failure and defeat in your life. In fact, there appears to be quite a lot written on the subject of Christian cursing and vindictiveness, with two of the prime sources being the passages from The New Testament (*Mark* 11.25 and *Matthew* 21-22) wherein Jesus placed a curse on a fig tree!

And on the morrow, when they had come out of Bethany he [*Jesus*] hungered. And seeing a fig tree afar off having leaves, he came, if perhaps he might find anything thereon: and when he came to it, he found nothing but leaves; for it was not the season of figs. And he answered and said unto it, 'No man [*will*] eat fruit from you from now on – forever.' ... And as they passed by in the morning they saw the fig tree withered away from the roots ...

Needless to say, theologians will put all manner of spin on the passages to show that Jesus didn't really destroy the tree (and someone else's property) in a fit of pique, but we can't escape the fact that he *did* throw a curse at the tree, even if it was merely to demonstrate a point.

7. The Conjuration of Destruction (Satanic)

In pure Hammer House of Horror purple prose, we turn to another curse from Anton LaVey's *The Satanic Bible*. On the surface, this conjuration may appear ludicrous and a trifle over the top, but performed under the right circumstances, it can work.

BEHOLD! The mighty voices of my vengeance smash the stillness of the air and stand as monoliths of wrath upon the plain of writhing serpents. I become as a monstrous machine of annihilation to the festering fragments of the body of she/he who would detain me.

It repenteth me not that my summons doth ride upon the blasting winds which multiply the sting of my bitterness; And great black slimy shapes shall rise from the brackish pits and vomit forth their pustulence into his/her puny brain.

I call upon the messengers of doom to slash with grim delight this victim I hath chosen. Silent is that voiceless bird that feeds upon the brain-pulp of him/her who hath tormented me, and the agony of them shall sustain itself in shrieks of pain, only to serve as signals of warning to those who would resent my being.

Oh come forth in the name of Abaddon and destroy him/her whose name I giveth as a sign. Oh great brothers of the night, thou who makest my place of comfort, who rideth out upon the hot winds of Hell, who dwelleth in the devil's fane; Move and appear! Present yourselves to him/her who sustaineth the rottenness of the mind that moves the gibbering mouth that mocks the just and strong! Rend that gaggling mouth and close his/her throat, Oh Kali! Pierce his/her lungs with the stings of scorpions, Oh Sekhmet! Plunge his/her substance into the dismal void, Oh mighty Dagon!

I thrust aloft the bifed barb of Hell and on its tines resplendently impaled my sacrifice through vengeance rests!

8. To Cross an Enemy (African)

This African curse demands rather a lot of mental application since it is set to work across nine consecutive days, and over a given period of time. You will also need access to a graveyard as the fetish will have to be buried where it is unlikely to be disturbed. Neither do you wish to draw attention to yourself while the rite is being performed. To perform the rite you will need the following:

One black figure candle (male or female as appropriate)
A needle or toothpick to mark the candle
Anointing oil of a Saturnian nature
Graveyard dust
A small box
Black cotton fabric
Cotton twine
Two silver coins
A small bottle of rum

Carve the name of your enemy into the candle and anoint the candle with appropriate oil. Gently sprinkle the candle with graveyard dust and make sure that any excess dust is contained within a clean cloth and does not get spilled in the house, as this could be counter-productive. Curse the person, wish them ill, or whatever as you coat the candle with the graveyard dust.

Light the candle for 17 minutes each day for nine consecutive days and keep it in a place where it cannot be touched or handled by someone else. After the ninth day, place the remainder of the candle in the box. Wrap the box in the black cloth and tie with the cotton twine. Take it to a cemetery and bury it. Pay the 'spirit' with whom you are burying the box the fee of two silver coins, together with the bottle of rum. Cover and conceal the 'grave'. Walk away without looking back.

9. The Curse of Cain

In Christianity and Judaism, the 'curse of Cain' and the 'mark of Cain' refer to the passages in the *Book of Genesis* where God declared that Cain, the firstborn son of Adam and Eve, was cursed for murdering his brother, and placed a mark upon him to warn others that killing Cain would provoke the vengeance of God. Oddly enough, the curse focused strictly on neutralising the benefits of Cain's primary skill – that of cultivating crops – and promised 'vengeance seven times over' should anyone kill him.

Nevertheless, Cain is associated with the 'magical arts', and features in Italian witchcraft, Romany magic and folklore, as well as the esoteric orders of Freemasonry. Daniel A Shulke writing in *The Cauldron* says: '*as an inheritance of both orthodox and heretical Christianity, it is also likely that the entrance of the figure of Cain into esoteric magical practice followed the route of the medieval Christian 'mystery plays' which experienced a high degree of development in Britain.*'

10. The Curse of Falling (or Drowning)

This rather unpleasant curse apparently has its origins in southern France but it was adapted for my book *Traditional*

Witchcraft for the Seashore, to cause drowning. The original was for broken limbs to be sustained during a nasty fall.

Go down, go down, my pretty youth,
But you will not come up
Tangled mind will twist and turn
And tangled foot will follow.
You will go down, my pretty one,
But you will not come up again.
So tangle, tangle, twist and turn,
For tangling webs are woven.

For the curse to be effective, something belonging to the victim is essential: you will need to obtain hair, nail clippings, saliva (not so easy these days with self-adhesive envelopes and stamps!) or skin. Handwriting is also a potent ingredient. Photographs help to focus the mind during spell casting and can be cut according to the damage you wish to inflict on the victim. If you cannot obtain anything that has been touched or belongs to the victim, then you will have to create some form of handwritten focus that includes their name.

You will also need some form of receptacle to contain the curse once the working is complete. Bear in mind that you will need to put this near the victim's place of residence, so it will need to be as unobtrusive as possible and in keeping with the surroundings. To charge the spell or curse, place all the items on a clean plate or tray and as you begin the chant, put them one by one inside the container having passed them through incense smoke (Air), over a candle flame (Fire), sprinkled with salt (Earth) and splashed with Water.

11. Curse From Beyond the Grave

This poem from Robert Herrick's *Hesperides* is a curse on a betraying lover or spouse that reaches out from beyond the grave. Aimed at a *'perjured man'* (i.e. someone who had broken a blood or sacred oath), and reliant on the perpetrator returning to the scene of the betrayal, this is very much the romantic cursing of bitterness rather than revenge.

> ### The Curse
> *Go, perjured man, and if thou e'er return*
> *To see the small remainderers in mine urn,*
> *When thou shalt laugh at my religious dust.*
> *And ask, Where's now the colour, form and trust*
> *Of woman's beauty? And with hand more rude*
> *Rifle the flowers which the virgins shrewed;*
> *Know, I have prayed to fury that some wind*
> *May blow my ashes up, and strike thee blind*

Like many classic poems, however, the above can be adapted into a workable curse by taking the last two lines to use as a repetitive chant. This should be accompanied by the writing of the victim's name on clean paper and sprinkling with graveyard dust – an important ingredient in many spells.

12. The Curse of Ham

The 'Curse of Ham' is derived from the Biblical story of Noah. Taken literally from the Old Testament text [*Genesis* 9:21-27] the characters have no racial or geographical identity but this 'ingenious Jewish tall tale' [Hon. Min Louis Farrakhan] is at the root of racism and white supremacy throughout the world.

> Even the most vociferous of the defenders of rabbinical honour, admit that the Talmudic rabbis had a 'preference' for light skin and that their stories 'see dark skin as a form of divine punishment'. One author believes that the motive of the Talmudic rabbis in promoting their version of the Curse was to justify the ancient Hebrew enslavement of the

Canaanites. What is not in dispute, however, is the ready acceptance of this racist construct by nearly every religious philosophy, culture and tradition on earth to justify their mistreatment of the Black race.

Ham was traditionally a dark-skinned son of Noah and the alleged founder of the North-Eastern Africans who spoke a language distantly related to Semetic. The Curse (or Hamitic Myth) has been hi-jacked 'whenever historical circumstances required the aggressive re-assertion of white supremacy' and can be shown to be at the root of the so-called 'justification' of the slave trade, and the displacement and murder of the Native Americans.

Jewish merchants and travellers of the 12th century denigrated the 'sons of Ham' in their writing as they opened up commercial interests around the known world. As a result, many races have adopted this myth of 'the chosen people' including the Puritans, the Jews, the Boers, the Afrikaners and the Nazis. The slave trade within the Islamic world put the Curse to full use, and Islamic clerics expounded on the curse of 'blackness', while colonial missionaries thundered it from American pulpits – North and South.

As a fine example of cursing and hexing, the Curse of Ham must surely be the most powerful of all, and demonstrates 'how a tiny Talmudic kernel can be made the universal creed'. Whatever spell or curse is cited to demonstrate the wickedness of witches, it would pale into insignificance when compared to this ancient by-product of the three monotheistic religions: Judaism, Christianity and Islam.

13. The Curse of the Hell Hounds

Also known as the 'Curse of Macha' and adapted from the version in E A St George's booklet, *The Book of Ghastly Curses*, this appears to be a very old witches' curse that calls upon the spectral Hell (or Gabriel) hounds who normally accompany the

Wild Hunt. These ghostly hounds are a widespread and integral part of British native superstition to such a degree that the mournful howl as an omen of death has almost reached the status of cliché in folklore writing.

Anyone who has ever heard the 'music of the hounds' will, however, understand the significance of this curse, since it comes in the form of a hunting. The victim experiences the sensation of being harried and pursued, especially during the hours of darkness, and the fear of being torn apart. Ideally it should be placed during the dark of the moon, or on a moonlit night when the clouds are scudding across the sky. In other words, on the type of night when the Wild Hunt would ride out.

Gather up a magic spell, summon forth the hounds of hell,
Over sea and over land, answer to a witch command,
Changing moon from bright to dim,
the hounds of hell must follow him.

Gather up a magic rite, hounds of hell go forth tonight,
Follow him where he shall go, follow hounds, the witch's foe,
Where he lies the blood will mark.
Changing moon from bright to dark.

Gather up a magic spell, follow him, O hounds of hell,
He who betrays must bleed, hounds of hell behold the deed,
Changing moon from bright to dim,
the hounds of hell shall follow him.

14. The Curse of Kaskaskia (Native American)

Dates from 1735 when a young Indian man was drowned in the river by a local fur trader for seducing his daughter. The couple had eloped but the trader and a group of friends set about hunting them down, resulting in the death of the Indian. Before he died, the boy 'threw' his curse ... that the trapper would be dead within the year; that he and the girl would be reunited forever in death ... town of Kaskaskia would be damned and destroyed, along with the land around it ... the altars of the churches would be destroyed and even the dead would be disturbed in their graves.

Within a year, the curse began its work. The girl pined away and died; the trader was killed in a fight. The river channels shifted, flooding the land, and by 1881 the town was completely cut off from the mainland. Homes and farms were abandoned; the church was moved again and again until, in 1973, the altar was destroyed in the flooding. By then, Kaskaskia had become a ghost town ... but not before the cemetery was washed away and the bodies of those buried there erupted to the surface and then vanished beneath the river.

15. The Curse of Nine (Witchcraft)

This traditional 'ladder' begins with a small affliction and finishes with death itself. The repetitive chant uses cumulative magic and would be mumbled under the breath as each knot was securely tied. The knotted cord would then be concealed about the property of the one cursed and allowed to work its magic – unless the 'ladder' could be found and the knots untied, the spell would run its course.

> *Ane's name*
> *Twa's some*
> *Three's a pickle*
> *Four's a curn*
> *Five's a horse-lade*
> *Six'll gar his back bow*
> *Seen'll vex his breathe*
> *Aught'll bear him to the ground*
> *And nine'll be his death.*

If we go back to the original textbook of medieval curses, the *Malleus Maleficarum*, we will find that curses were used not only against people but also against buildings and livestock. Almost any local misfortune could be laid at the door of witchcraft and the whole text of the *Malleus* is littered with uncorroborated and repetitive accusations. Here we have it in chapter and verse that *'there is no bodily infirmity, not even leprosy or epilepsy, which cannot be caused by witches …without the use of any poison, but by the mere virulence of their incantations, they can deprive men of their lives'*.

By contrast, it is interesting that very few contemporary books on witchcraft even bother to mention cursing. Even Margaret Murray in *The Witch-Cult in Western Europe* and *The God of the Witches* makes do with a few quotes from the classic witch-trials, while Gerald Gardner in *Witchcraft Today* wrote that he knew of no spells to do people harm. Most writers steer clear of the subject … which is odd because modern books are full of beneficent spells and charms. Odd … because if a witch is capable of laying a spell to heal, by qualification s/he *must* also have the power to curse.

There are often crimes that go unpunished and here the witch has recourse to a 'Higher Law', which allows a perpetrator to be dealt with magically. In *The Book of Ghastly Curses*, E A St George cites this method: 'The most effective is as follows: Construct a simple code based on the person's name. Write out the appropriate curse in that code, using a slightly disguised handwriting. Put the curse into an envelope and see that it falls into the hands of the person for who it is intended.'

16. The Curse of the Smith

In *White Horse: Equine Magical Lore*, Rupert Percy cites 'The Curse of the Smith' for use against anyone harming or attempting to harm a horse.

May their skull be crushed as the iron is crushed by the hammer.

May their bowels be torn as the iron is seized by the tongs.
May their blood spurt from their veins as the sparks fly from beneath the hammer.
May their hearts freeze from cold as the iron is cooled in water.

This curse is used to cast a spell over people who are unknown, and who may be some distance away from the sender. The only equipment you need is a horseshoe nail, which should be bent and twisted with a hammer and pliers, held in the candle flame and plunged into a bowl of water, using the above chant as you do so. In view of the savage and brutal attacks often made on horses and ponies, surely there would be few who would object to such a curse being laid at the perpetuator's door.

17. The Curse of Tecumseh (Native American)

The origins stem from the fact that since 1840, all US Presidents who have been elected in years ending in zero, have been killed or have died in office. And the one exception came literally within an inch of death. This eerie co-incidence is purported to be traced back a Shawnee chief who cursed the 'Great White Fathers' following his defeat at the hands of William Henry Harrison at the Battle of Tippecanoe in 1811. Tecumseh died two years later at the Battle of the Thames, again fighting troops led by Harrison.

Another version attributes the curse to Tenskwatawa, tribal medicine-man and half brother to Tecumseh, who 'threw' it to revenge the death of his half-sibling. *'Harrison will die, I tell you. And after him, every Great Chief chosen every 20 years thereafter will die. And when each one dies, let everyone remember the death of my people.'*

18. The Cursing Doll

A doll found buried in Hereford in 1960 was the effigy of someone whom a local witch once cursed, for tucked into its skirt was a spell that read:

> *I act this spell upon you from my whole heart, wishing you to never rest nor eat nor sleep the restern part of your life. I hope your flesh will waste away and I hope you will never spend another penny I ought to have.*

The doll is now in the Hereford City Library Museum, but the text suggests that the effigy was created by someone who knew what to do … but not how to do it!

19. The Cursing Pot (Welsh)

A fine example of a Welsh cursing pot can be seen at Gwynedd Museum and Art Gallery, Bangor, which was found in 1871 by a labourer carrying out maintenance work at Penrhos Bardwyn Farm on Anglesey. A piece of local slate tile had been placed over the top of a small black pot or 'pipkin'; on both sides of which was scratched the name 'NANNY ROBERTS'. Inside the pot were the remains of a frog, and it was evident that several large pins had been stuck into its body, suggesting that the pot was used as part of a ritual curse.

According to the accompanying museum text, it was customary for folk who wished misfortune against another person to stick pins into a live frog then place it in a pot, along with the name of the person to be cursed. The curse would remain in place, until the victim was able to find the pot; even if the frog was burnt in a house fire the curse was not nullified. In some areas it was deemed unlucky to kill a frog, so the curse couldn't be lifted, because it involved the sacred elements of blood and iron.

To bring the curse up to date, substitute a piece of fresh meat and stick it with pins before placing it inside a small jar. This spell then becomes a 'bottling' and can be undone at any time. Scratch the name of the intended victim on a small piece of slate or tile and use it to cover the jar, whilst chanting over and over the type of misfortune you wish to inflict on them. Conceal the jar near the victim's home – traditionally burying it near the path where they will walk every day.

20. The Cursing Well

Although wells are usually visited for their healing properties, there are exceptions; the most famous being the 'cursing well' at Llanelian-yn-Rhos in Denbighshire, Wales. To bring misfortune upon someone it was believed that if their name was written on a piece of paper and given to the well's custodian they would be cursed. For a 'small consideration', the custodian would wrap the paper around a stone and drop it into the water.

In 1929 the well was covered over but it was believed that the malediction would only be effective as long as the paper survived in the well. According to *Folklore, Myths & Customs of Britain (Reader's Digest)*, the custodian was usually open to cash inducements to retrieve the names of those who believed a curse had been laid upon them. Although thought of as a curse, this is more of a binding spell, since the 'curse' could be undone by the retrieval of the paper, with the belief that the curse was only effective as long as the paper remained intact and did not disintegrate in the water.

21. The Death Curse (Templar)

The public death of the Grand Master of the Knights Templar, Jacques de Molay, gave rise to the legend that he had called down a curse on the King of France and his family for thirteen generations, and on the pope who had condemned the holy order in a betrayal of God's trust. He called upon King Philip IV and Pope Clement V to meet him within the year before the throne of God to answer for their crime. The Pope died during the following month, to be followed seven months later by Philip IV. The curse finally burned itself out upon the death of the Royal family during the Terror.

Jacques de Molay's death was particularly vicious, even by medieval standards. The pyre was constructed from carefully selected cured wood and charcoal to produce a slow-burning fire of intense heat that would roast the condemned men from the ground up, to prolong their lives and their agony for as long as possible. Not surprisingly, the Grand Master's curse demanded death in recompense for the indignities heaped upon the Templars.

Someone who had exhausted all reasonable avenues of resolution, and who now appealed to a Higher Law threw this more focussed death curse. Interestingly, the origins of this curse are totally ambiguous in terms of religious belief ...

I call down death upon thee ,[Name]
Death be thy portion and the grave thy home.

Because thou hast done evil and stopped up thine
ear to counsel, or reason, it is my desire that thy name
shall be blotted out from the Roll of Life.

Die then, and let thy memory be no more.
So mote it be!

22. The Egyptian Curse

Cursing was common in ancient Egypt, according to Geraldine Pinch in *Magic in Ancient Egypt*, where red pots on which Execration Texts were written were ritually broken as part of the cursing ceremony in order to smash an enemy's power. It was the words spoken that accompanied the actions performed during the dedication rite that actually inflicted the curse.

'The Cursing Litany', translated by Margaret Murray, is probably the most deadly of all, because it is not only aimed at the living, but also the obliteration of a person's spirit and memory after death. For the ancient Egyptians, to deprive someone of their Name was to rob them of a continued existence in Amenta (Otherworld). This particular curse requires the participation of two or more people: one to speak the curse, the other(s) to repeat the refrain *'Mayest thou never exist'*.

Mayest thou never exist, may thy ka *never exist, may thy body never exist.*
Mayest thou never exist.

May thy limbs never exist.	*Mayest thou never exist.*
May thy bones never exist.	*Mayest thou never exist.*
May thy words of power never exist.	*Mayest thou never exist.*
Mayest thou never exist.	*Mayest thou never exist.*
May thy form never exist.	*Mayest thou never exist.*
May thy attributes never exist.	*Mayest thou never exist.*
May that which springs from thee never exist.	
	Mayest thou never exist.
May thy hair never exist.	*Mayest thou never exist.*
May thy possessions never exist.	*Mayest thou never exist.*
May thy emissions never exist.	*Mayest thou never exist.*
May the material of thy body never exist.	*Mayest thou never exist.*
May thy place never exist.	*Mayest thou never exist.*
May thy tomb never exist.	*Mayest thou never exist.*
May thy cavern never exist.	*Mayest thou never exist.*
May thy funeral chamber never exist.	*Mayest thou never exist.*
May thy paths never exit.	*Mayest thou never exist.*
May thy seasons never exist.	*Mayest thou never exist.*
May thy words never exist.	*Mayest thou never exist.*
May thy enterings never exist.	*Mayest thou never exist.*
May thy journeying never exist.	*Mayest thou never exist.*
May thy advancings never exist.	*Mayest thou never exist.*
May thy comings never exist.	*Mayest thou never exist.*
May thy sitting down never exist.	*Mayest thou never exist.*
May thy increase never exist.	*Mayest thou never exist.*
May thy body never exist.	*Mayest thou never exist.*

May thy prosperity never exist. *Mayest thou never exist.*
Thou art smitten, O enemy.
Thou shalt die, thou shalt die.
Thou shalt perish, thou shalt perish, thou shalt perish.

The more people there are taking part in the rite, the greater the impact, because the voices resonating the refrain will create a truly magically potent chant. The Egyptians never did anything by halves and if using this curse it is ideally placed under formal conditions by a group of people who are directly affected by the victim's actions that warrant such an extreme response.

23. The Exeter Curse

Another example of how much more virulent and indiscriminating a Christian curse can be, is one is adapted from the *Exeter Book*, a collection of writings given by Bishop Leofric, between 1046 and 1073AD, to the library of Exeter Cathedral. It is still one of its treasures. Nearly all First English writing deals with the life of Christ, legends of the saints, or otherwise directly religious in its nature. 'The Fortunes of Men' reveals from this early date how the 'hellfire and damnation' curse would be hurled, not only at the sinner, but anyone connected to them by blood or friendship. Here a family's sons die one by one:

One the wild wolf shall eat.
Hoary hunter of the wastes.
One shall sharp hunger slay.
One shall the storms beat down.
One shall be destroyed by darts [arrows].
One die in war

One shall live losing
The light of his eyes.
Feel blindly with fingers.

And one, lame of foot
Wearily wasteth away
Musing and mourning
With death in his mind.

One, failing feather,
Shall fall from the height
Of the tall forest tree.

One shall go grieving
One the great gallows
Shall have in its grasp
Strained in dark agony
Till the soul's stay,
The bone-house, is bloodily
All broken up;
When the harsh raven hacks
Eyes from the head.

One shall burn in the bale-fire
The bright cruel flame.
Shall devour the man destines
To die in its maw.

One shall die by the dagger
In wrath, drenched with ale.
Wild through wine, on the mead bench,
Too swift with his words

One killed by himself

Any of the above could be used as a curse in its own right, except that many of the activities that proved so fatal at the time the *Exeter Book* was written are obsolete today. A violent drunkard, however, could still fall victim to the 'dagger', as knife-crime appears to be on the increase!

24. The Gage, or Challenge

An interesting adaptation from the Walter de la Mare poem and used in revenge for the killing (or deliberate injuring) of a pet dog, *The Gage* offers an example of an extremely powerful curse. For example:

> *O mark me well!*
> *For what my hound befell*
> *You shall pay twenty-fold,*
> *For every tooth*
> *Of his, i'sooth,*
> *Your life in pawn I'll hold.*

Here we are bringing down a curse that is **twenty times** the number of teeth in the dog's mouth, which for an average healthy, adult dog is around 42. This means that the magical practitioner must weigh in the balance whether the punishment fits the crime. After all, it would be rather extreme if someone had merely given your dog a clout for attempting to ravish their prize-winning bitch! That said, this curse used against any act of cruelty against a dog – intentional or unintentional – might be seen to be justifiable. Cursing, like most areas of magic, is a question of personal responsibility and/or morality but once thrown cannot be retracted.

For this particular curse it is necessary to produce two separate pouches: one containing the fur, etc. of the dog and the other, the items relating to your victim, rendered down into ash, whilst reciting the curse. The pouch containing your canine bits and pieces will be retained and kept somewhere safe. The pouch containing the actual curse can be emptied in the victim's garden, posted through their letterbox, sent through the post, or handed to them in person. Remember that even the mildest accident magnified 20 x 42 is going to have *serious* repercussions!

25. The Gypsy's Curse

Fortune telling and the provision of charms, love potions and herbal remedies are part of the gypsy way of life. Gypsies, or more correctly, the Romany have always been veiled by an aura of mystery. They began to move into Europe in the 14th century and the enigma of their origin, the romantically nomadic way of life, and their supposed magical powers, have surrounded them with a lasting aura of fear.

Gypsies are generally deeply religious, but their religion operates on two separate levels. They share the religious observances of the local non-gypsy community, but also have traditional rituals of their own. Gypsy folklore encompasses belief in many kinds of supernatural events, powers and creatures and, to combat them, various kinds of magic are used either to circumvent evil forces, or on occasion actually inflict ill upon others.

This traditional gypsy curse has chilled Europeans for years, as it reflects the rootless way of life that has been forced on the Romany throughout history.

> *May you wander over the face of the earth forever,*
> *never sleep twice in the same bed,*
> *never drink water twice from the same well,*
> *and never cross the same river twice in a year.*

Authentic 'gypsy curses', however, are probably few and far between. One quote on the subject may be nearer to the truth ... 'The curses are one of our secrets. If the *gaje* wish to learn of them they can ask one of us in person. We might tell about them, then again we might not, and then we might make up something ... for isn't that what the *gaje* say of us? Let them find out the truth by experience. You ask can they remove it? If they talk to the gypsy king/queen, or possibly the bandolier. Those are the only ways to remove the curse once it is upon them. Either that, or kill themselves ...'

26. The Græco-Roman Cursing Tablet

One of the most common methods of cursing in the ancient world was the use of lead tablets, known in Greek as *katadesmoi*, and in Latin as *defixiones*. These cursing-tablets appear to have been a specifically Greek invention, known in Greece from the 5th century BC and spreading throughout the Mediterranean world. The earliest ones consist merely of a victim's name, scratched on a thin sheet of lead and thrown into graves, pits, or wells, thereby consigning the victim to the 'care' of chthonic forces. As time went on, these tablets became more elaborate, with long texts and intricate designs, and their preparation often entailed complex rituals. As is indicated by the Latin term of *defixiones*, iron or bronze nails were often used to pierce the metal tablet after it had been rolled or folded.

To date, more than 1,500 examples of curse-tablets have been excavated: of these, two-thirds are Greek and over half of the Latin examples have been found in Britain. Most were excavated at the Temple of Mercury at Uley in Gloucestershire and the sacred spring of Sulis Minerva at Bath, so the practice appears to have been imported into Britain at the time of the Roman invasion. Traditionally, lead was the common metal used, and the place for depositing the curse-tablet was almost as important as the text itself, because 'the 'magic' could only be initiated by the *defixiones* being buried in either a grave, a chthonic sanctuary, a body of water, a place of relevance to the curse victim ...'(*Phases in the Religion of Ancient Rome*, Cyril Bailey)

The older the tablets, the simpler the inscriptions, and the majority from the 4th-5th century BC make no mention of deities or spirits, giving only the name of the intended victim. By the 1st century AD formulaic instructions were being added and while later they became far more brutal, in the classical period, curse-tablets were designed to incapacitate the victim rather than kill. Some feature names written backwards, with the letters facing right, or with the words written in a spiral, in order to mystically change or 'scramble' the victim.

The following example is from a curse-tablet found at Minturna. It was written in Latin but contains many misspellings, which has led to the probable conclusion that it is the work of someone from the lower classes. The glee that it takes in thought of Ticene's misfortune, and the thorough way in which every single part of her body is listed as a potential site for pain (even her shadow) demonstrates the depth of feeling experienced by the perpetrator:

Spirits of the underworld, I consecrate and hand over to you, if you have any power, Ticene of Carisius. Whatever she does, may it all turn out wrong. Spirits of the netherworld, I consecrate to you her limbs, her complexion, her figure, her head, her hair, her shadow, her brain, her forehead, her eyebrows, her mouth, her nose, her chin, her cheeks, her lips, her speech, her breath, her neck, her liver, her shoulders, her heart, her lungs, her intestines, her stomach, her arms, her fingers, her hands, her navel, her entrails, her thighs, her knees, her calves, her heels, her soles, her toes. Spirits of the nether-world, if I see her wasting away, I swear that I will be delighted to offer a sacrifice to you every year.

[Jo-Anne Shelton, *As the Romans Did*, OUP]

As most authors of curse-tablets seem to have preferred not to name themselves, it can only be presumed that they feared the repercussions of the curse. Another point to be taken into account is that the *defixiones* were usually hidden in earth or water since their power was dependent upon their not being discovered.

An ideal modern substitute for lead would be the dull side of heavy-duty baking foil, with the curse being 'written' into the metal using a blunt pencil. The foil can then be folded or rolled, and pierced with a nail, before being concealed in a suitably secure place in close proximity to the victim. The use of aggressive language also appears to play a significant part in this method of cursing but again, be warned … this is an authentic and extremely ancient system of cursing and should not be undertaken lightly.

27. The Hag Stone Curse

This is an interesting protective curse, which was used in a racing yard when it was discovered that someone was interfering with the riders' tack. One work rider was always assigned an extremely dangerous horse as the first ride out of the morning and it was discovered before leaving the yard (and crossing a busy main road) that both buckles had been undone on the bridle and carefully looped back, so that the pin did not go through the leather. Any pressure on the bridle and the reins would have come away in the rider's hands.

This action was tantamount to severing the brakes on a car, as the horse was a known rogue and needed all the rider's skills to keep it steady. Had it played up when crossing the road, there could have been a dual fatality. Unfortunately, there was no way of knowing for sure whom the perpetrator was and so the following curse was thrown in the tack room:

Let the hands that do the mischief,
be the hands that take the fall

Suspicion had fallen on one particular person who had left another yard after a similar incident, but from that day the rider kept a hagstone in their bag, and silently repeated the curse each time they entered the tack room, whilst holding the hagstone.

Eventually, the person who had been suspected took a nasty fall on the gallops and was injured so badly that they could not continue working in racing.

Whether the malicious actions of the perpetrator were meant as a joke is immaterial, sooner or later there would have been a serious, if not fatal, accident. Making the curse general, rather than aiming it at an individual, safeguarded the *sender* from targeting the wrong person.

28. The Irish Curse

Even the most dire of curses can contain an element of humour as these two examples from Ireland show. With a little bit of imagination the first can be utilised to expose an enemy.

May those who love us, love us
And those that don't love us,
May God turn their hearts.
And if He doesn't turn their hearts,
May he turn their ankles,
So we'll know them by their limping.

Or for more drastic measures:

May his pipe never smoke, may his teapot be broke
And to add to the joke, may his kettle ne'er boil,
May he keep to the bed till the hour that he's dead,
May he always be fed on hogwash and boiled oil,
May he swell with the gout, may his grinders fall out,
May he roll howl and shout with the horrid toothache,
May the temples wear horns, and the toes many corns
Of the monster that murdered Nell Flaherty's drake.
May his spade never dig, may his sow never pig
May each hair on his wig be well thrashed with a flail,
May his door have no latch, may his house have no thatch,

May his turkey not hatch, may the rats eat his meat
May every old fairy from Cork to Dunleary,
Dip him snug and airy in river or lake,
Where the eel and the trout may feed on the snout
Of the monster that murdered Nell Flaherty's drake.

Irish curses have a simple logic all of their own but even those tinged with humour in the original, can be extremely effective when empowered in magical terms.

29. Irish Cursing Stones

Both these Irish curses were listed in *The Penguin Guide to the Superstitions of Britain and Ireland* by Steve Roud.

Fire of Stones

The first is a power procedure, usually carried out by tenants forced to leave a farm against their will, and involved placing a curse on the land by building a fire of stones:

The victim collects from the surrounding fields as many large stones as will fill the principal hearth of the farm he is being compelled to surrender. These he piles in the manner of turf sods arranged for firing; and then, kneeling down, prays that until the heap burns, may every kind of sweat, bad luck, and misfortune attend the landlord and his family, to untold generations. Rising, he takes the stones in armfuls and hurls them here and there ... in loch, pool, bog-hole or stream, so that there is no possibility that they can all be recovered.

Some regional details vary and in some cases the stones are left in the fireplace, to increase the dramatic effect. The incoming occupant will be left in no doubt as to what has been done. Sometimes an eggshell full of water was placed on top of the stones to suggest that the ill luck would last until the stones boiled the water.

Turning the Stones

'Turning the stones' was a way of inflicting a potent curse on anyone you wished to harm. The Co Cavan 'cursing stone' is a large horizontal slab, with 12 or 13 basins: in each basin (except one) there is a large round stone. The curser takes up one of the stones and places it in the empty basin – and so on, until all of them have been moved.

During the operation he is cursing his enemy and if he moves all the stones without letting one slip (not easy on account of their shape and size), his curse will take effect, but not otherwise. If he lets one slip, the curse will return on his own hand.

30. Lancashire Death Spell

Elizabeth Southern, better known as 'Old Demdike', confessed to witchcraft at the Lancaster Assize Court in 1613, explaining one method by which witches believed they could commit murder. She declared that in order to kill someone by sorcery, witches would …

> … *Make a Picture of clay, like unto the shape of the person whom they meant to kill, and dry it thoroughly, and when they would have them to be ill — and … have any part of the body to consume away — then take part of the Picture and burn it. And when they would have the whole body to consume away, then take the remnant of the said Picture and burn it, and so thereupon by that means the body will die.*

The case of the Lancashire witches is England's best documented witch trial thanks to Thomas Potts, who was the Clerk of the Court at the hearing and afterwards used his records to produce *The Wunderfull Discoverie of Witches in the Countie of Lancaster*, published in 1613.

31. A Lover's Curse (Witchcraft)

Usually one steeped in vengeance and revenge, and the required outcome is that the jilted lover has the satisfaction of making sure those responsible for his/her unhappiness do not find it with each other.

I [… Name …] make this philter.
May it bear malediction,
Deep affliction,
Here upon this pair,
… [Name] … and … [Name] …
May they never be united,
may they quarrel every day,
May their bond be blighted
Before the year has passed away!
This shall be the life between them,
Let that life be as it may!

So mote it be!

For the curse to be effective, something belonging to both parties is essential to the successful preparation of the philtre. For this you will need to obtain hair, nail clippings, or skin from both, placed in a sealable jar containing brine. Photographs help to focus the mind during spell casting, especially if both parties are together in the same picture, as their images can be separated by cutting as part of the spell. If you cannot obtain anything that has been touched or belongs to either party, then you will have to create some form of handwritten focus that includes their names, and which can be separated during the working.

Take two lighted candles – one white and one gold – place the white one to your left and the gold one to your right. To charge the spell, place the items you intend to use on a clean plate or tray and as you begin the above chant, cut the images apart. Using the white candle, burn the image representing the female party and the gold candle to burn the other half representing the male. Keep the philtre jar somewhere safe, so that you can give it a vicious shake from time to time, but dispose of the two sets of ashes by flushing them down the lavatory – separately!

32. The Nemean Curse

The curse-tablets or *defixiones* of the ancient world give an incredible insight into the religious beliefs and magical practices of the time. The following example is from a Nemean curse-tablet, dated to the late 4th century BC. This separation spell, written by a jealous or spurned lover, was found with five others by the same individual, and is interesting to archaeologists because it refers to homosexual relations, and also because it makes no mention of spirit or deity in the text.

I turn away Euboles
from Aineas, from his
face, from his eyes,
from his mouth,
from his breasts,
from his soul,
from his belly, from
his penis, from
his anus, from his entire body.
I turn away Euboles from
Aineas

People confided their feelings in the tablets as they would be loath to do to a companion or friend, and the picture they paint of life is an incredibly vivid one. The actual wording of the text reveals far more about their authors than simply whether they were copying from another standard tablet. Once placed, the tablets were hidden by earth or water since their power was dependent on their not being discovered or removed. That the curse-tablets worked (or were seen to work) is demonstrated by the large numbers of people who used them and obviously believed in the outcome.

33. Nidstang or Nithing Pole (Norse)

Nidstang means, literally 'curse pole', or the Nithing Pole – 'riding pole', and is an ancient Scandinavian custom of a formal curse. According to Norse sources, a 'nithing' was a person who has forfeited all honour and respect because of their deeds, and would be cursed as a result.

A wooden pole or stake was inscribed with spell-working runes and the intended result, and erected publicly with all due ceremony. A horse's head or carcass was placed atop the pole facing in the direction one wished to send the curse, and the animal's hide spread on the ground. The concept behind the pole was that it would terrify and drive away the offender's guardians, which in turn would lead to ill-fortune on the one cursed. 'To place a 'nid' on someone was a form of verbal curse, a magic ritual that was considered very powerful during the Viking age. The power of words was not taken lightly, so a curse of this kind was something very serious to send, not to mention having a 'nid' spoken over oneself,' writes Darryl Trainor, an authority in Norse folklore.

Some sources suggest that the pole was cut from a hazel tree and symbolically this rite suggests that the spirit of the horse would carry the curse, swiftly and directly, to the person for whom it was intended. In olden times, it would have meant the ritual slaughter of a horse but today we can implement the use of imagery and construct our 'horse' from other materials ... i.e. a small bag stuffed with horse hair, resembling a horse.

34. Pointing the Bone (Aboriginal)

A traditional Aboriginal curse is placed by 'pointing the bone' publicly at the victim. Traditionally the bone should from an emu or kangaroo and 'pointed' in order to bring that person ill fortune, or even death. This is an extremely effective curse, with strong psychological overtones because the sender does not speak as the bone is pointed. The fact that the curse is thrown before witnesses gives it even greater power, and there have been many recorded occasions when victims have just lain down and waited to die after being cursed.

35. The Poppet

The Museum of Witchcraft in Cornwall has a large collection of poppets used for cursing. The companion booklet states that the most effective method of cursing is to use a poppet (doll), fashioned in the likeness of the individual then ritually harmed, usually by stabbing with pins. A witch would incorporate an object that belonged to the victim within the poppet, to makes the curse especially effective. One of the poppets on display has human pubic hair sewn into place while others have nail parings.

This 'murder by image-magic' is an extremely old and potent form of magic and provided a safe and simple method of killing the victim, because it could be carried out from a distance. It is also a universally common practice of creating a likeness to represent another person, and is recorded by Sir James Frazer as 'an attempt which has been made by many people in many ages to injure or destroy an enemy by injuring or destroying an image of him, in the belief that, just as the image suffers, so does the man, and when it perishes he must die.' [*The Golden Bough*]

One of the examples cited was taken from the North American Ojibway tribe … 'He makes a little wooden image of his enemy and runs a needle into its head or heart, or he shoots an arrow into it, believing that wherever the needle pierces or the arrow strikes the image, his foe will the same instant be seized with a sharp pain in the corresponding part of his body; but if he intends to kill the person outright, he burns or buries the poppet, uttering certain magical words as he does so.'

Generally speaking, the poppet resembling the victim can be made of clay, rags, wax or wood and given the name of the victim. To be *really* effective a wax poppet should contain nail parings, hair, spittle, semen, shred of clothing, etc., to represent every part of the victim's body. According to the nature of the curse, it could be pierced with nails, pins or thorns; melted slowly before a fire, or held over a lamp every night for seven nights, saying:

> *This is not wax that I am scorching*
> *It is the heart, liver and spleen of ...... that I scorch.*

After the seventh night, burn the figure and the victim will die. This method of cursing combines the principles of both *homoeo-pathic* and *contagious* magic, since the image was made in the likeness of the victim and contains materials that had been in contact with him (or her).

Another form of disposal is to bury the poppet, preferably in the middle of the path where the victim must step over it. One curse even has a cop-out of laying the blame on the shoulders of the archangel Gabriel, who is considered to be a great deal better at bearing the responsibility than the perpetrator!

> *It is not I who am burying him,*
> *It is Gabriel who is burying him.*

In some cases the poppet can be placed in running water, but whatever method is used, the effect on the human victim is the same.

36. Psalm 109

Curses are available to all and sundry and need no more special powers than the necessary degree of anger or spite. Even so, there was always the warning that a curse uttered lightly, or performed badly, would rebound on the curser. This version was recorded in Wales by Trevelyan in 1909: *'Any person can pray that his enemy be dead, if he wishes to repeat Psalm 109 every night and morning for a whole year. If he misses one night or morning, he must certainly die himself.'*

Psalm 109

Hold not they peace, O God of my praise;
For the mouth of the wicked and the mouth of the
*   deceitful are opened against me:*
They have spoken against me with a lying tongue.
They compassed me about also with words of hatred;
And fought against me without cause.
For my love they are my adversaries:
But I give myself unto prayer.
And they have rewarded me evil for good,
And hatred for my love.
Set thou a wicked man over him:
And let Satan stand at his right hand.
When he shall be judged, let him be condemned:
And let his prayer become sin.
Let his days be few ...

The complete text for Psalm 109 can be found in any edition of the Bible.

37. Pure Poison

Unlike the 'Curse From Beyond the Grave' (which is *very* specific), the following is the belt and braces approach in that *nothing* is left to chance. Only to be used in extreme circumstances, it leaves the outcome wide-open to Fate. Every aspect of magic has its positive-negative aspects and this curse calls upon the negative powers of the elements.

May you be struck down by the poison of Earth
May you be struck down by the poison of Air
May you be struck down by the poison of Fire
May you be struck down by the poison of Water

Only to be used when life is threatened because it can spill over to affect others in close proximity to the victim and *cannot* be controlled once thrown. For example:

Earth: Poisonous plants and minerals
Air: Poisonous gas
Fire: Poisonous fumes or smoke inhalation
Water: Contaminated water or seafood

This curse is giving complete freedom of action on the psychic planes to use any and every means to 'take out' your enemy. This means that the sender must have no qualms about the outcome should the curse affect other members of the victim's family, etc. In other words, the curse should not be used indiscriminately or frivolously, or out of spite, as there *will* be a price to pay.

38. A Rival's Curse

This curse is another adaptation of a poem by Walter de la Mare and can be used to destroy the physical charms of a rival. Beauty is, of course, in the eye of the beholder, so the destruction does not need to be a physical attack on the victim, but the lessening of their charms in the eyes of the lover. There are, however, two points to ponder:

- If the curse is being sent through sheer malice with the ultimate aim of bringing about the destruction of a *sanctified* partnership, then it would be going against the free will of the lover. Even though this may undertaken in the guise of a 'love spell', it is technically an act of 'black magic' in terms of magical morality ... **and there will be a price.**

- If, on the other hand, we are looking at opening a lover's eyes to the wiles and guiles of our rival, then we are actually focussing our attention on stripping away a false front.

The Song of the Secret

Where is thy beauty?
Gone, gone:
The cold winds have taken it
With their faint moan;
The white stars have shaken it,
Trembling down,
Into the pathless deeps of the sea:
Gone, gone
Is beauty from thee.

Sprinkle white rose petals or orange blossom with salt and seal in an air-tight container as you recite the charm; keep for two of the moon's quarters: from the half to the dark of the moon. By then the petals should have begun to wither and these can be scattered on the rival's property.

39. The Scottish Curse

Curse on the English read by Scottish priests following the closing of their religious houses c1530:

I curse their head and all hairs of their head. I curse their face, their eyes, their mouth, their nose, their tongue, their teeth, their shoulders, their back, and their heart, their arms, their legs, their hands, their feet, and every part of their body from the top of their head to the soles of their feet, before and behind, within and without ...

I curse them walking, and I curse them riding. I curse them eating, and I curse them drinking. I curse them within the house, and I curse them without the house. I curse their wives, their bairns, and their servants ...

I curse their cattle, their wool, their sheep, their horses, their swine, their geese, and their hens. I curse their halls, their chambers, their stables, and their barns ...

This classic example of a thoroughly Christian-based curse, which leaves no stone unturned is, again, far more vicious and far-reaching than many Craft-based versions. Few witches would feel the need to extend a curse to include family members and livestock, since a traditional 'witch's curse' would normally be directed at someone doing them (or theirs) ill.

In Christianity there appears to be no governing lore relating to the placing of curses, regardless of the severity, but it must be admitted that the above must have been an extremely alarming text when it was delivered from the pulpit during the 16th century.

40. The Sporting Curse

It is known that sportsmen of the Roman world used 'defensive phylacteries and spells' to counter any *defixiones* that may have been directed at them. Secrecy was paramount with more underhand curses, such as those made against rival charioteers, and in 389AD the *defixiones* were made illegal under Roman law. Clearly, the psychological power of these tablets was immense.

The following is a 75-line curse-tablet found in Carthage. The author 'appears to be erring on the side of caution', and cursing every single horse of the Red and Blue teams, along with their drivers – yet despite this attentiveness to detail, he does not know the name of the dead soul to whom the job is entrusted.

I invoke you, spirit of one untimely dead, whoever you are, by the mighty names SALBATHBAL AUTHGEROTABAL, BASULTHATEO SAMABETHOR bind the horses whose name and images [or likeness] on this implement I entrust to you; of the Red [team]: Silvanus, Servator, Lues, Zephryus, Blandus, Imbraius, Dives, Mariscus, Rapidus, Oriens, Arbustus; of the Blues: Imminens, Dignus, Linon, Paezon, Chrysaspis, Argutus, Diresor, Frugiferous, Euphrates, Sanctus, Aethiops, Praeclarus. Bind their running, their power, their soul, their onrush, their speed. Take away their victory, entangle their feet, hinder them, hobble them, so that tomorrow morning in the hippodrome they are not able to run or walk about, or win, or go out of their starting gates, or advance either on the racecourse or track ... [*Learning From Curse Tablets: What Defixiones Tell Us of the Ancient World : website*]

41. *Tabellae Defixionum*

That spells (*carmina*) and curses (*dirae*) were not figments of poets imagination, but were in current use in Rome, there is ample evidence both in literature and in the *tabellae defixionum* that have been found – mostly in graves. It is also clear that in Roman magic, even more than in Greek, it was the words, or rather the 'singing' of the magic chant (*carmen*), that was the important and efficacious part of the rite.

In the inscriptions that have come down to us the *carmen* is usually associated with the magic rite of *defixio*, or 'nailing' – where the wax image of the person to be affected was either pierced with a needle or burned in a fire. The intention of this process was not to harm an enemy, but to secure a reluctant lover's affection! In other cases, however, the object is clearly to bring harm to a personal enemy and the following is to bring about the effect of mutilation of an image by mentioning all the parts of the victim's person and his possessions:

The eyes, hands, fingers, arms, nails, hair, head, feet, thigh, belly, rump, navel, chest, breasts, neck, mouth, cheeks, teeth, lips, chin, eye [sic], forehead, eyebrows, shoulder blades, shoulder, nerves, bones, marrow, stomach, leg, money, profits and health of Nico, I, Malcio, nail on to this tablet.

[*The Religion of Ancient Rome,* Cyril Bailey]

42. The Wedding Curse

Not everyone wishes the bride and groom well on their wedding day, and rival lovers had traditional ways of venting their anger or jealousy. Psalm 109 is looked upon as a means of destroying forever the fortunes of a young couple if read by a rival during the marriage service. The Psalm is pretty powerful stuff when read with a vengeful tongue.

Other magical rites were possible: If anyone at a marriage repeats the benediction after the priest, and ties a knot at the mention of each of the three sacred names on a handkerchief, or a piece of string, the marriage will be childless for fifteen years, unless the knotted string is burnt in the meantime.

A jilted person can wait in the church porch until the bridal couple appears and then throw a handful of rue at them saying: 'May you rue this day as long as you live.' It is important that the curse be thrown in the porch because the rue has been taken direct from the plant to the church and thrown between holy and unholy ground' – i.e. between the church and the churchyard.

43. The Widow's Curse

This is one of the most powerful curses to be laid at anyone's door and is usually thrown following the persecution or harassment of a defenceless widow. The following examples, one from folklore and the other from Irish history demonstrate that simple god-fearing Christian folk do have the power to curse. The lyric for the folk-song *Widow's Curse* tells of the curse thrown by a mother at the seducer of her daughter, following the girl's suicide.

Upon her knees her mother fell; to heaven did cry and call
'If ever widow's curse,' quoth she, 'on mortal man did fall,
Then say amen to mine, Oh Lord, that he may never thrive
Who was the cause of this sad fate but not rot away alive'
His nails from out his fingers fell, his eyes from out his head
His toes they rotted from his feet before that he was dead
His tongue that had false sworn so oft to compass his desire
Within his mouth did swell and burn like coals of sparking fire
And thus in torment for his sins the wicked villain died
Whose hateful carcass after death could not in earth abide
But in the maws of carrion crows the ravens made their tomb
And then in hell he screamed and writhed in everlasting doom!

When Sir Robert Gore Booth was landlord over a part of Sligo c1839, the worst evictions that ever took place in Ireland were those of the 'Seven Cartrons' in the parish of Drumcliffe, where about one hundred families were evicted in the one operation. The landlord wished to take over the land for a grazing ranch for his cattle and shipped the families off to America. Those who stayed were lucky, for the rotten ship sank with all hands on board. The name of the ship was the *Pomano* and at the time there was a song composed with many 'cursing' verses ...

My curse be on Sir Robert and that he may lie low
Our rent was paid we were not afraid
But still we were forced to go
When they banished the Roman Catholic
Aboard the Pomano.

Reminiscent of the Highland Clearances in Scotland, when people were evicted to make way for sheep, the events of 1839 in Ballygilgan are well remembered. Having decided to make clearances on his newly acquired property, Sir Robert secured the services of Captain Dodwell, who was even then notorious in the area for his ruthless evictions. Folk memory has it that the reason for the forced removals was that …

Lissadell House was just built. Ballygilgan was too close to it and his wife didn't like the smell of the turf-smoke coming from the cottages. Houses were demolished, roofs torn off, walls thrown down. The scene was frightful; women running wailing with pieces of their property and clinging to door-posts from which they had to be forcibly torn; men cursing, children screaming with fright. That night the people slept in the ruins, next day they were driven out, the foundations of the house was torn up and razed.

Amidst the fallen roof timbers and broken walls of her home an old woman went down on her knees to curse her persecutors. *'The 7th Baronet will never reign,'* she swore, *'the Gore-Booths will melt from the face of the earth.'*

Sir Robert was the 4th baronet, Sir Henry the 5th and Josslyn was the 6th,' a local man who heard of the incident recalled. 'Twas the widow's curse' he said 'that was known in me father's an' in me grandfather's time. They knew all about that from one generation to another. And it has come to pass! The 7th Baronet was a Ward of Court; he suffered from mental illness his whole life, he never reigned. How d'ye explain that?

With the sale of Lissadell House in 2003 the Gore-Booth presence in Sligo has indeed come to an end. It happened exactly as the distraught and destitute old woman predicted so many years before!

Let the Curser Beware!

We don't really know where the word 'curse' comes from … type in the word on the Internet and you'll find that most of the listings are to do with swearing or foul language, rather than anything of a magical bent. Some suggestions trace it back to the Anglo-Saxon *curs*, an 'imprecatory prayer' or malediction, the primary meaning of the word being the prayer or calling itself.

In truth, a malediction and a curse are not precisely the same thing and to be completely accurate – as one should always be in matters of magic – the action of malediction is in the uttering of a curse. 'Diction' means speech or speaking but can also mean the 'rendition of words in singing, as regards to pronunciation', according to an entry in an old *Webster's Dictionary*. B R Gendler [*Curses & Maledictions*] takes this examination even further: 'The first component of the word, *mal*, simply means bad or evil … putting these components together we see that a 'malediction' is a *calling of evil upon someone*'.

Gendler continues: 'It should be worthy of note that the result of a 'curse' or 'malediction' is a *malifice*. The former two words really pertain to the incantation itself, but the *effect* of such is a 'malefice'. If one puts a curse or spell on someone, which is not based on utterance, but on action – such as a poppet or so-called voodoo doll, it should properly be referred to a *maleficiation*. The action of placing a maleficiation on someone is to 'maleficiate', which more simply means 'to make evil'.'

It should also be remembered that the deliberate use of magic to inflict harm is a universal feature of the religion and folklore of almost every culture in the world.

Some sources believe that the victim should be made aware that they have been cursed, so that their own fear will lend additional power to the curse. Others believe that victims should be kept in ignorance so they will not attempt to propitiate the evil force in some way.

The far-reaching effects of a curse were brought home to the people of Carlisle, following the installation of a piece of art in the form of the 'Cursing Stone'. The stone, a 14-ton granite slab intricately carved with a 16th-century diatribe against the border raiders of the period was intended as a community art project to honour the city's colourful past, and commissioned by city counsellors for the Millennium celebrations. Created by Carlisle-born artist Gordon Young, the Stone now stands at the centre of the city, near the castle.

The 1,069-word curse was originally levelled at those 'reiver families', who regularly raided Carlisle and other parts of northern England from just over the border during the 16th-century and was placed by Gavin Dunbar, Archbishop Glasgow, in 1525. Since the 'Cursing Stone' was installed, however, Carlisle suffered the worst local flooding for more than a century, which killed three people; an outbreak of foot and mouth, and a succession of local job losses as factories closed ... even the football team was relegated from the Football League! As a result, the local council debated whether to move the Stone outside the city boundaries, or even destroy it altogether.

There are claims that the placing of a 'non-Christian artefact, based on an old curse on local families, had brought bad-luck to the city' but the original was a *Christian* curse, which could now be seen to be re-activated by the number of people becoming aware of it, and moving or destroying the Stone won't necessarily change Carlisle's fortune. The artist is an actual descendant of one of the old reiver families, and this blood link, coupled with the curse being made public again, means that the roots now go very deep. The present Archbishop of Glasgow has been asked to 'lift the curse', but perhaps he should bear in mind that *re-channelling* or *re-directing* a curse is the only way to get rid of it, for once placed, it cannot be lifted ...

Traditionally, it *can* be returned to its sender! This process requires something from the person *placing* the curse, with the name of the sender written on a piece of paper and then burnt in a metal container, with these words:

Three blows hast thou dealt;
By evil heart, evil eye and evil tongue.

These same three blows be thine own reward!
By fire and water, earth and air,
And that which binds and governs them
I charge the touch him/her not!

... but should the curse be sent back to Gavin Dunbar, who was, after all, only taking the necessary steps (as he saw fit at the time) to protect the people of Carlisle from the vicious attacks of the Scottish borderers? There is no answer, but it should be obvious that no curse should be an impromptu, knee-jerk affair ... even if you are a member of the Christian clergy, or the instigator of a community arts project!

Binding & Bottling

Many people confused binding and bottling and, although similar in preparation, the long-term outcome is often employed for different purposes. Neither carry the finality or strength of a full-blown curse and, unlike the curse, both can be 'undone' should it become necessary to negate the spell for whatever reason.

- Bottling is used long-term to contained both positive *and* negative energies, and is a method that can be traced back to ancient Egypt. The witch-bottle can be placed in the walls of a house for protection; as an amulet; or as a container for the negative energies of an enemy. **Time limit: indefinite.**

- Should the matter require less drastic measures than cursing or bottling, we can use a binding spell to prevent someone from carrying out some unwise action. When the moment of madness has passed, the binding can be undone. **Time limit: short duration.**

Curses, in the long term, are usually counter-productive and self-defeating, since few people who throw a curse bother to concern themselves with the far-reaching implications. Binding and bottling give a far greater 'control' over the outcome and if, at the end of the day, you decide it's really not worth the effort, then the bottling or binding can be undone … **a curse cannot.**

The Witch Bottle

Numerous examples of 'witch bottles' have been found in old houses during modern renovations. The Reigate Witch Bottle, for example, was found buried in a ruined house. The bottle was complete and the stopper was still in position, which provided archaeologists with the opportunity to examine the contents. In this case, the bottle itself was rather old, having been made about 1685, but it was not buried until sometime after 1720, so it was already 40 years old when it was utilised for spell casting. Prior to burial, it had been well used, with chips on the rim, and had been re-used year after year for containing wine or other liquids. When it was discovered and the contents analysed, it was found to contain urine.

A similar find occurred at the Lincolnshire village of Navenby, where a witch bottle was discovered buried in the foundations of a rural farmhouse. Dated to around 1830, it contained bent pins, human hair and perhaps urine and was probably a glass inkwell or candlestick. The house's new owner has decided that it should go on display at the Museum of Lincolnshire Life rather than replacing it in the foundations.

The outsider's interpretation often claims that witch bottles were used as a protection *against* witches when, in fact, they could have had several uses. The whole idea of a witch bottle is that it will act as a container for either positive or negative energies ... depending on the original purpose of the charm. It was customary to bury one as a *protective* device under the hearth or under the doorstep to prevent bad luck entering the house ... bottles were also plastered into the walls and hidden in attics ... and often had very little to do with witchcraft.

By disposing of a witch bottle that has been concealed *inside* a house, the current owners could be throwing away the building's protection, which will have increased with the years. The sensible occupant would be well-advised to re-bury the bottle as near to the initial site as possible and thereby retain the luck and good wishes that originally went with it. Whenever one of these artefacts is discovered, the popular press, and even archaeologists, will insist that the bottle was targeted *at* a witch, and will even go so far as to advise on how to kill the suspect by preparing your own witch bottle! And they say witches are dangerous!

Bottling

Needless to say, not all witch bottles are benign in origin, and any found inside the perimeter of a property's boundaries ... especially next to a well-used path ... should certainly be treated with some degree of suspicion. Each 'bottling' is prepared in a very personal way, and even though the contents may appear sinister or malevolent, this may not necessarily be the case. Since the bottle is meant to represent an individual, then some of that individual's personal DNA will have gone into it – whether for protecting or controlling purposes. But even a protective charm for a new house needs some careful thought and preparation because that may turn into a curse, if not properly thought out.

For example: the well-meaning witch decides to make a witch bottle as a protective gift for a newly married couple. In among the rusty nails and bent pins intended to keep negative forces at bay, she includes snippets of hair from both the bride and groom. The witch bottle is carefully concealed in the new house and forgotten about. The years pass and the couple begin to grow apart; they would like to separate but 'something' ties them together ... Since this book is about cursing, we will not concern ourselves with protective rites – but do be warned. Strangely enough, the ingredients for a protective charm are almost the same as for a bottling, so make sure you get it right!

- The use of bent pins and nails harks back to the use of iron to negate negative energies and in later times, iron was said to repel the Faerie Folk, who often paid nocturnal visits to human communities. Iron has always been considered to have durable magical qualities and was originally used to make nails, particularly horseshoe nails – pins were a substitute when iron was no longer available.

- Blackthorn spikes do not have any beneficial qualities in terms of bottling, and the inclusion of these in a charm would confirm that there was malevolence afoot. *Anyone who has had a wound caused by a blackthorn will know just how painful even the slightest scratch can be.*
- Broken glass and razor blades are other hostile ingredients that would rarely be found in protective bottlings.
- Personal items such as hair clippings, nail parings and saliva are essential for any successful bottling – positive or negative.
- Photographs or handwriting are utilised to personalise a charm.
- In magic, urine has a dual purpose. It can be used as a method of 'marking a territory', or as a sign of contempt.
- Blood is, of course, the most potent substance that can be used in magic, and it depends on the proposed outcome as to whether fresh blood or menstrual blood is used. *The addition of fresh blood (a pin prick on the finger will suffice) is the ultimate magical seal on a charm. Menstrual blood is a negative addition that renders something (or someone) impotent or sterile.*
- Plants such as nightshade, hemlock, aconite, etc., can also be added to the bottle, depending on the required outcome of the charm. Witches have long been known for their knowledge of poisons and the addition of a natural plant extract to a bottling will have the same effect as though the victim has swallowed it – even if it's only the leaves of the common stinging nettle (picked after July) to induce stomach cramps and diarrhoea!

1. A Charm to Bring in the Witch

If we find ourselves under some form of magical attack from another witch this bottling charm, written by Robert Herrick, could be used against the instigator. Witches are notoriously jealous of those who suddenly demonstrate genuine psychic abilities and it's not uncommon for someone to find themselves the victim of these unwanted attentions for no other reason than pure malice. This charm quoted in *Traditional Witchcraft for the Seashore* is a method of preparing and using a witch bottle against one of your own kind, should it become necessary.

A Charm to Bring in the Witch

To house the Hag, you must doe this;
Commix with Meade a little Pisse
Of him bewitcht: then forthwith make
A little Wafer or a Cake;
And this rawly bak't will bring
The old Hag in. No surer thing.

Urine is a powerful ingredient in magical preparations and a true witch will not shy away from using it. Here, it is used as part of the charm to deflect 'bewitchment' or psychic attack by 'bottling' the sender's energies. For added protection, and also to act as a 'binding' spell on the perpetrator, it would be a good idea to place the wafer or cake inside a small glass bottle or jar that can be sealed tight. Keep the jar in a place of discomfort, i.e. the freezer, in the coal shed, outside lavatory, etc.

If the victim feels further twinges of discomfort, he or she should shake the jar vigorously in order to upset the equilibrium of the sender. And don't be too eager to dismantle the jar if the sender suddenly appears to have had a change of heart – it's much easier to keep the bottle 'on hold' than it is to redo the charm, because it will never have the same potency the second time around.

2. To Control a Wandering Spouse or Partner (Voodoo)

Aimed at curtailing the amorous wanderings of a legitimate spouse or partner, rather than a casual romance that has gone sour. For this reason the bottling will be made more potent by using your own bodily fluids to 'fix' the spell. For this rite you will need the following:

A red candle
A blue candle
Candle holders
A gold wedding ring
A 6-inch or larger round mirror
Purple fabric large enough to cover mirror
Parchment paper, Dove's Blood Ink and a quill pen
Incense burner and charcoal
Incense and incense powder
Twine or red cord
Scissors
A large sealable jar
A needle or other sharp instrument to inscribe your candles.
3 personal items from your lover: Hair from head or pubic region, a small piece of underwear and small piece of worn sock or stocking
2 anointing oils: one drawing – one commanding

Place the mirror on your altar and cover with purple fabric. Place the wedding ring in the centre as a symbol of your promise of unending love, and prepare appropriate incense. Using a sharp implement, mark both red and blue candles with the name of your lover. Write his/her name all over the surface and inscribe his/her initials in any spaces the whole name will not fit. Once finished, dress the blue candle with the oil – anointing the candle from base to wick. Dress the red candle in the same fashion. After you finish each candle, consecrate it to the appropriate 'spirit' or speak your intentions aloud.

The blue candle forces your lover to bend to your will. The red candle is a symbol of your demands. Light both candles and place them in their respective holders. Light the incense and begin the ritual by removing the red candle from its holder. Slowly drip the wax into the centre of the ring, focussing on what you want from your relationship. Once the ring is half full, repeat the process with the blue candle. This time, speak your lover's name and command him/her to act in the fashion you desire. Replace candles and allow them to burn out completely.

When the ring is full and the wax is cool, remove from the ring. Begin kneading the wax and forming into a ball shape. As you do this, add your lover's personal items to the wax. Focus on kneading them, forcing them to your will. See him/her acting the way you want. Visualise the relationship the way you want it to be. When finished, hold the ball with both hands and recite Psalm 126 three times.

- Cut the parchment paper in half. Using the quill, write a petition of your desires for the relationship in Dove's Blood Ink on one half of the paper.
- On the other half, write both of your names, cutting around the names in the shape of a heart.
- Now lay your petition down on the mirror (still covered with the purple fabric).
- Place the heart in the centre of the petition; place your wax ball on the centre of the heart and sprinkle the ball of wax with a commanding powder.
- Wrap the ball of wax up in the petition paper.
- Form the paper around the ball of wax so that the bottom remains in a round shape and then twist the excess at the top.
- Wrap the purple fabric (that is covering the mirror) around this packet in the same manner.
- Tie it off with the twine or red cord.
- Wrap the twine or cord around the packet several times and visualise tying the force or power of the packet within

itself.

- Knot this string nine times and trim off any excess fabric/string.

At this point, you have several options. To make the bottling stronger, you might masturbate yourself to completion and anoint the bag with your fluids. Or you could anoint the bag with your own urine (taken before dawn and before you have spoken to anyone). Using personal bodily fluids within magical working is far more powerful than relying on commercial or artificial ingredients.

- If you anointed the bag with your own sexual fluids, also rub nine drops of the 'commanding' oil into the bag.
- If you anointed the bag with urine, also rub nine drops of the 'drawing' oil into the bag.
- If you did neither, rub nine drops of both oils into the bag.

Fumigate the bag completely with incense. Pray for the spirit or your deity to grant your wishes and control your wandering lover. Place the bag on the mirror and let it sit there until the candles burn out; put the bag inside the jar and place underneath your bed on the side you *don't* sleep. This symbolises the place you want your lover to stay. You might light a purple candle weekly and hold the jar over the flame – heating it up while praying for your desires. Keep the bag anointed with oil to maintain its affects.

In the event of your lover returning, do not be tempted to undo the bag and disperse the contents. There's nothing wrong with the belt and braces method, so keep it secret, keep it safe.

3. To Get Rid of an Enemy (Voodoo)

An enemy is one who wishes us harm and so a bottling is carried out in order to minimise the threat. Although this magical approach is not as strong or as irreversible as a curse, the likelihood of being able to retrieve it is doubtful. You will need:

1 black candle
1 small dark coloured bottle with cap
Commanding oil
Banishing powder
Black coffee (brewed very dark and strong)
Small piece of brown paper (a torn grocery bag will do)
Black cotton fabric
Cotton twine
A needle to mark the candle

Using the needle, carve the name of your enemy all over the candle and when you run out of space for the whole name use the initials. Anoint the candle with the commanding oil and gently dust the candle with banishing powder. Do this by taking a tip of a spoonful of the powder and blow gently onto the candle. Light the candle and begin working on the bottle as follows:

- Write the person's name nine times on the brown paper.
- Roll the paper away from you into a tube shape and slide it inside the bottle.
- Add nine drops of oil and a nice pinch of the powder into the bottle.
- Then fill with the coffee until the bottle is full.
- Weight the bottle, close and seal it with wax from the candle.
- Wrap the bottle in black cloth.
- Tie with cotton twine making nine knots using all the anger and rage you can muster.
- Take the bottle to a body of moving water.
- Toss into the water over your left shoulder and walk away without looking back.

4. To Get Rid of an Troublesome Neighbour (Voodoo)

Neighbour disputes are on the increase and this bottling spell is designed to remove the problem without the need for *you* to move house. Because this is classed as an 'enemy working', it will be necessary to cleanse yourself thoroughly each night after you perform the rite. Prepare consecrated water sufficient for nine nights and mix with hyssop; recite Psalm 51 at the end of each spell cycle.

It is advisable to work somewhere where no one will touch the bottle or candle, preferably outside and away from your own home. Be careful when handling the ingredients and wear disposable gloves when handling the materials. Cover the working space with newspaper or black bin-liners as you do not want any of these ingredients accidentally getting into your house by mistake, or you may be the one who is moving out! You will need the following materials and equipment:

1 black image candle (male or female to represent neighbour)
1 jar banishing incense
Banishing powder
Banishing oil
Cayenne pepper
A needle to mark the candle
Incense burner and charcoal
Large bowl or plate
Small piece of brown paper
Soil from the neighbour's garden, or a personal item
Consecrated water
Disposable gloves
A glass jar

Using the needle, carve the name of your neighbour all over the image candle and when you run out of space for the whole name, use the initials. Baptise the candle by sprinkling it with consecrated water and saying *'I name you* [Name] *in the name of the Father, and the Son and the Holy Spirit'*. Begin by calling the candle by the neighbour's name. Visualise the candle as that person.

Now turn the candle upside down and make a small hole in the bottom; insert either dirt from the person's yard or a personal item. Anoint the candle with the oil, from the bottom to the top. Talk to the person, telling them they will be too uncomfortable to stay in their home any longer – that they *must* move away. Tell them you are covering them with disharmony so they will no longer find peace and happiness in their home. Turn the candle right side up and stand it in the centre of a large bowl or plate. Gently dust the candle with the banishing powder by taking a spoonful and blowing gently onto the candle. Sprinkle cayenne pepper on the candle's head.

On the same evening as you prepare the candle, begin burning incense for the spell. Place the incense burner directly in front of the candle (which should be on a plate or in a bowl). Light the charcoal and write the person's name 27 times (9x3) on the brown paper. Using your thumb, mark an 'X' over the person's name with the oil, and repeat that they will be very uncomfortable staying in their home; and that the only way to resolve it is to move out! Be creative and give them a list of problems they will have: skin crawling, nightmares, things bumping in the night, fighting with family members, etc. Trace this 'X' with the banishing powder and fold it.

Next, add the banishing incense and begin by making your prayers for the person to move. You may choose to say the following portion of Psalm 68 nine times.

God arises,
His enemies are scattered
and those who hate Him flee before Him,
As smoke is driven away, so are they driven;
as wax melts before the fire,

so the wicked perish at the presence of God.

As you do, add a sprinkling of banishing powder to the incense. Be careful here! This powder will pop, crackle and produce much smoke. Drop the name paper onto the incense and let it burn. Extinguish the candle.

Repeat the procedure with the incense and name paper for nine nights in a row. Each morning, rise and speak to no one. Take a spoon and scoop up some of what is left in the incense burner and sprinkle it on top of the image candle. On the ninth night, burn your incense and light your candle (by now it should be thoroughly covered with powder and charcoal soot.) Make your prayers and allow the candle to burn all the way out. You must stay awake for this! Once the candle has been completely consumed, take the remaining wax and begin making 13 small pellets or balls.

Take the remainder of what is in the plate or bowl, wrap it in brown paper and place inside the jar, sealing it tightly. Go to the crossroads and dispose of the jar over your left shoulder. Walk away and do not look back. On your way home, throw the 13 wax balls onto the neighbour's roof. As the sun rises it will melt the wax and make it impossible for the inhabitants to stay in the house.

5. The Guilt-Dream Bottling

A bottling for someone who has betrayed us, or let us down badly on the romantic front (i.e. a former spouse or lover), using the poem *Ever* by Walter de la Mare as the repetitive chant. Again we are using repetitive lines to build the power as the rite is carried out. Since this is not a destructive charm, and obviously geared to pricking the conscience of the 'lost love' with a view to drawing them back, the bottle should include the petals and thorns of a rose.

At the full moon, under the hour of Venus, prepare the witch-bottle by combining the rose petals and thorns with personal items from the missing lover or a photograph. Complete by adding sweet wine as you chant:

Ever, ever
Stir and shiver
The reeds and rushes
By the river:
Ever ever,
As if in dream,
The lone moon's silver
Sleeks the stream.
What old sorrow,
What lost love,
Moon, reeds, rushes,
Dream you of?

If possible, try to prepare the witch-bottle outside, where the light of the moon is reflected in the surface of the water. If there is no safe access to a river, use a garden pond or fill a wide, shallow dish with water and position it where it can reflect the light of the moon. Conceal the witch-bottle somewhere safe out of doors and repeat the charm periodically at different phases of the moon.

6. The Money Bottle (Voodoo)

This money drawing spell can apparently *'be 'fixed' by burying it close to your home, as an alternative to actually keeping it in the house'.* In fact, it would have the *opposite* effect and any money coming to you would stop at the door! There should be no reason for a money bottle to be buried outside the home as the intension is to draw prosperity *inside*. You will need:

5 cloves
5 cinnamon sticks

5 kernels of dried corn
5 kernels of dried wheat (or 5 teaspoons wheat flour)
5 pennies
5 10p pieces
5 20p pieces
5 sesame seeds
5 pecans
5 whole allspice

Put the ingredients into a jar, making sure the top is secured tightly. Shake the bottle vigorously for five minutes while chanting words such as:

Money gain, silver and herbs
Copper and grain hear my words

Place the money bottle somewhere safe in your home where no one can interfere with it. Leave your purse or wallet near the bottle when at home.

7. To Stop Harassment

Designed to stop harassment and send the one doing harm as far away as possible. Should be done ideally on a Saturday when the Moon is in her dark phase. Items needed:

3 black candles
Black thread
Parchment or clean paper
An item from the perpetrator
A small piece of black cloth
A screw-top jar

The three black candles should be placed in a triangle, designating the area in which the spell should be worked, with one point facing North. Light the candles and sit for a moment, meditating on the result that is required. Write the name of the person who is causing grief on the paper, draw a cross through the name and fold it three times three, saying:

Leave [Name] *well alone*
You are removed from causing harm in any way.
Get out of [his/her/my] *life*
And let [him/her/me] *be free from this day.*

Take the paper and personal items, and wrap them in the black cloth, before binding them three times three with the black cord, chanting as you bind:

With this cord I bind and fix the spell
Go forth now and speed it well.

When the cloth is bound tight, put it in the jar and screw the lid on as tight as possible. Blow out the candles, then take the jar and bury it as far away from the victim's home as possible. When this has been done, relight the candles and allow them to burn out.

8. The Tanglefoot Charm

To prevent someone from carrying out an action, one of the best methods is a variant of the spell known to many practitioners as *The Tanglefoot Charm*, quoted in full by Paul Huson in *Mastering Witchcraft*.

Obtain a link object from your victim, either a strand of hair, which you must plait into a cord with some red twine, or an article of clothing in which you can comfortably tie knots. On a night when the moon is waning, preferably a Saturday midnight just before the new moon, cast your triangle with a Saturnian fumigation, having bitter wine in the chalice, and stones, twigs and bones upon your altar. In the triangle place the specially prepared cord. Invoke the dark power, using the circle crosses and the counter-clockwise [widdershins] circumambulation and when you feel that chilly, numbing presence is at hand, only then begin your spell.

Take the cord in your left hand (always the left hand for operations of darkness), and tie nine deliberate knots in it, starting with one at either end and working inwards. As you do so, chant this incantation, employing your imagination to strongly visualise the result of your spell upon the victim. *See him unable to speak or perform whatever the action is you wish to prevent.*

[Name] *I conjure thee,*
by night your eyes are blinded!
By clay your ears are stopped!
By earth your mouth is sealed!
By rock your limbs are bound!
Having tied the last knot, chant, *'So mote it be!'*

Take the knotted cord, place it in a sealed bottle, and bury it in the ground near where your victim lives or walks. If you do not live in close proximity, then find an inhospitable spot that will not be disturbed by a stranger. This is a symbolic funeral in order to heighten the charm and, because it is only a bottling (i.e. a holding spell), you must be able to retrieve it, if circumstances change. As you bury the bottle, chant these words as you do:

Twist and tangle [Name]
never to rise up again.
Your eyes are dimmed,
your limbs are bound.
Thus I lay you down to rest
still and silent in the ground!

When you wish to undo the charm, you must perform a ritual that does everything in reverse. Invoke the powers of *Air* to release the victim. Dig up the bottle on a Wednesday while the moon is waxing. Cast a circle, using a Mercurial incense, and invoke Herne with your square of Mercury. Begin by untying the centre knot and working outwards, in the reverse sequence you tied them in, chanting a jingle with each knot. While doing this, you must wield your powers of imagination to see the magical bonds falling from the erstwhile victim.

By winds your limbs are freed,
By the breath your mouth is opened,
By the words your ears are opened,
By the light your eyes are brightened.
[Name] I conjure thee,
Awake, arise; so mote it be!

This method, also known as ligature, is a comparatively mild method of chastisement and may be thought of as more in terms of a binding, except for the amount of time and effort needed for the operation. The charm has a long-term effect, and you would not put this amount of work into a binding, which is only short-term.

9. To Temper Ambition

Ambitious people can sometimes be a threat to a community or individuals in the workplace and this bottling can 'douse' those ambitious urges until the wider picture becomes apparent. The 'flesh on fire' is the burning, all-consuming ambition that needs to be checked and *'better 'tis that one should fall than by one hazard all'*. Assemble the following:

A small glass jar
A jug of rain water

A small square of paper
Pen and blue ink

Write the name of the troublemaker on the paper, using ink that will run when placed in water. Tuck the paper into the glass jar with the name showing through the glass. Pour in the water and, as you do so, repeat the following Herrick verse:

The Scar-fire

Water, water, I desire,
Here's a house of flesh on fire;
From the fountains and the springs,
And come all to bucketings.
What ye cannot quench pull down,
Spoil a house to save a town.
Better 'tis that one should fall
Than by one hazard all.

Each time the troublemaker manifests, give the bottle a good shake and repeat the charm. If the trouble persists, keep on shaking and chanting! Keep them bottled until the danger is passed and then tip the contents of the jar into running water.

The Binding

Binding is a form of short-term preventative magic inasmuch as the spell can be used to stop someone doing something foolhardy – such as taking out a loan they can ill-afford. It is not meant to be permanent and, unlike cursing or 'bottling' is easily reversed when the moment of madness has passed. For example:

Here today and gone tomorrow;
Nowt to buy with, nowt to borrow.
or
Rooted and bound; rooted and bound.

You are bound to me till a way be found

1. An Allay for Love

This rather unpleasant charm is a genuine 17th century spell for severing the affections of two people. Before we start, there should be the warning that if the separation goes against the free will, then this can most certainly be considered to be 'black magic' no matter how convinced we are that the cause is just.

If so be a toad be laid
In a sheep's skin newly flayed,
And that tied to man, 'twill sever
Him and his affections ever.

If, however, someone is willing to wear a dead toad wrapped in a smelly sheep's skin about their person, it must raise some serious questions about their own personal sanity!

2. The Binding by Hair

'Tis but silke that bindeth thee,
Knap the thread, and thou are free:
But 'tis otherwise with me;
You are bound, and fast bound so,
That from me you cannot go.

It was thought that witches could cause storms, raise tempests and generally wreak havoc with the weather by letting their hair flow loosely. In 17th-century Scotland, this was still a popular superstition and local women were prevented from combing their hair while their brothers were away at sea. It was also a belief that a woman was rendered powerless if she had no hair and it was for this reason that the Inquisitors shaved the heads of witches before torturing them.

Lovers often exchanged locks of hair as proof of devotion, for the simple reason that if one betrayed the other, the hair could be used in a spell against the unfaithful lover.

The Bondman

Bind me but to thee with thine hair,
And quickly I shall be
Made, by that fetter or that snare
A bondman unto thee.

Or if thou tak'st that bond away,
Then bore me through the ear,
And by the law I ought to stay
For ever with thee here.
Robert Herrick

3. To Bind an Enemy (Wicca)

If dealing with a real enemy, whose name we know, it may be necessary to bind them for a considerable amount of time. This Wiccan binding will last longer than normal but the natural symbolism behind the charm should not be lost on an experienced practitioner.

Gather cobwebs from your house or, if you don't have such things, collect them from a shed or outhouse. Now you will need a dead fly: one already entangled in the web would be perfect. Place them together on a small circle of black cloth, chanting as you do so:

North, South, East West,
Spider's web shall bind him [her] best.
East West North, South
Hold his [her] limbs and stop his [her] mouth
Seal his [her] eyes and choke his [her] breath
Wrap him [her] round with ropes of death

Fold a paper containing your enemy's name into four and wrap it, together with the fly and cobwebs, in the black cloth, forming it into a small pouch or bag. The opening should be bound with a long cord and suspended in a dark corner of the house where dust and cobwebs can gather, i.e. an attic or loft. Do not disturb but let it hang until it is thickly covered in dust. Then take it down and bury it in the earth to work its influence in perpetual secrecy as the cloth rot away.

The idea behind this binding is that as the spider 'saves' its prey until it is ready to deal with it, so you will be keeping a tight control over your enemy. Resist the urge to undo the binding unless you are 100% sure that the danger is passed.

4. To Bind Your Lover

This particular binding has all the sexual innuendo often associated with witchcraft and magic. For it you will need:

A red genitalia candle (male or female to represent your lover)

A black figure candle (male or female to represent your lover)

A length of black cord or cotton twine nine times longer than the genitalia candle

A needle to inscribe your candles.

3 personal items from your lover: i.e. hair from head or pubic region, nail clippings, a small piece of worn underwear, or a small piece of worn sock

Appropriate anointing oils

Take the red genitalia candle and, using the needle, mark it with the name of your lover. Write his/her name all over the candles. Place his/her initials in any spaces the whole name will not fit. Once finished, dress the candle with oil – anointing from wick to base. Take the black figure candle and mark it with the name of your lover in the same fashion. Once finished, dress the figure candle with the oil – anointing the candle from base to wick.

Focus and concentrate on the genitalia candle as if it was your partner. Envision him/her excited ... stroke it, play with it – get funky. Do your thing! Suddenly grab the cord and begin wrapping and tying the genitalia candle. As you twist the cord around the candle begin knotting it randomly – a total of nine times. Once completely tied up and bound, begin to burn the black figure candle. For nine minutes focus your attention on the genitalia candle, commanding that no pleasure will arise from it without your 'help'. When the rite is finished, pinch the candle out (*do not blow it out!*). Do this for nine consecutive nights.

Once the figure candle has burned out, keep the genitalia candle wrapped up in dark fabric and place it in a dark space, until you lover acts as you have commanded them. You can take the genitalia candle out and rework it with a new candle if your lover appears to be getting up to his/her old tricks.

5. The Bittersweet Binding

According to Culpeper, this plant *'is good to remove witchcraft both in men and beast, and all sudden diseases whatsoever'*. Magically, woody nightshade (*solanum dulcamara* or *amara dulcis*) can be used for a 'Bittersweet Binding' against someone who is gossiping about, or slandering you. This binding is a method of 'staying a poisonous tongue' since woody nightshade or 'bitter-sweet' is known to paralyse the central nervous system if taken internally. Here we use what is known as sympathetic magic, by binding the leaves or berries (both are toxic) of the plant, together with hair, nail clippings, saliva or a photograph of the guilty party. This preparation should be buried at the root of the woody nightshade with the demand that its poison shall still the gossiping tongue of your enemy

6. To Cause Impotency (Witchcraft)

The ability of witches to cause impotence in men was something that occurs again and again in accusations of *maleficia*. This was called 'ligature' – a state of impotence generally accomplished by tying knots in threads or through binding. The typical methods – *vaecordia* [Latin], *aiguillette* [French], or *ghirlanda delle streghe* [Italian] – were to tie knots in a cord or strip of leather and hide it. This 'detestable impiety', which merited a witch's death if the culprit could be discovered, would continue until the cord was found and untied; the ligature would remain permanent if the cord were not found, or if the knots could not be loosened. The incantation for the rite accompanying the knotting of the cord would be either the first, taken from *A Treatise of Magical Incantations* dated 1886:

> *Twine in three knots, Amaryllis;*
> *in three colours twine them,*
> *Amaryllis, do and say.*

Or in Scottish dialect from *Satan's Invisible World Discovered*, dated 1871:

> *Far si far, fa far fay u, far four na forty*
> *Kay u Mack straik it, a pain four hun*
> *creig wel Mack smeoran bun bagie.*

7. To Cause Impotence (Moroccan)

In the *Complete Book of Magic & Witchcraft*, Kathryn Paulsen gives this North African version: 'To make a man impotent, write an incantation expressing the result you desire on the blade of a pocket knife, or a pair of scissors. Shut it carefully and bury it in a deserted place where no-one will find it, for the charm will be broken if the knife is opened or the incantation removed.'

8. Commanding a Person (Especially for Money Owing)

Money is often the root cause of people falling out, and it is never easy to ask for the return of a loan, even if the borrower has exceeded the time stipulated for repayment. In business we make allowances for 'slow' payers, but if we find ourselves waiting months for settlement of an invoice, our own business may suffer. This binding is aimed at 'pricking the conscience' and astrally encouraging the debtor to make payment. For this binding you will require:

A purple candle
A small glass jar
A handful of pins
Frankincense joss
Coins to represent the debt
A written 'bill' showing the amount of the debt and the name
    of the debtor

Set the ingredients on a tabletop in front of you and light the purple candle on a Thursday night in the hour of Jupiter [for finance]. Burn the joss over a plate to gather the ash. Make your petition aloud, naming the debtor and the amount of the debt, before holding the written bill in the candle flame until all the paper is consumed. Collect all the fragments and mix with the ash from the joss. Taking the glass jar in your left hand (left hand for receiving) begin to add the pins and coins, saying as you do:

Be bound to me or pay the fine,
Pay what is mine,
Or only hardship will be thine

Repeat over and over again until the jar is full; add the frankincense ash from the joss and seal with purple candle wax. Shake the jar vigorously and do this periodically until the debt is paid in full.

9. The Greek Binding

Greek curses were common, but in most instances not meant to be fatal. The most frequent were 'binding curses', and among the most common artefacts are small pieces of lead, so thin that a simple stylus can be used to engrave a message upon them. Curses and love charms abound in this medium and these simple lead rectangles called *katadesmoi*, may originally have been more elaborate than the surviving metal. There is evidence of the casting of a 'thrice cold curse', which calls for the use of several colours of yarn to be plaited and knotted in an elaborate ritual manner and more perishable materials may have accompanied the surviving metal.

A recently discovered example came from a woman called Dagina, wishing to bind the man Dionysophon to her for life:

On the formal wedding of Thetima and Dionysophon I write a curse, and of all other women, widows and virgins, but of Thetima in particular, and I entrust upon Makron and the demons that only whenever I dig out and unroll and re-read this, then may they wed Dionysophon but not before; and may he never wed any woman but me; and may I grow old with Dionysophon, and no one else. I am your supplicant: Have mercy on your dear one, dear demons, Dagina, for I am abandoned of all my dear ones. But please keep this for my sake so that these events do not happen and wretched Thetima perishes miserably and to me grant happiness and bliss.

This is a fine example of an ancient binding curse because it seeks to control another person's behaviour and can be dug up and destroyed if the lady in question changed her mind.

10. The Lover's Chain

Most Roman love charms are either to cause the failure of a rival, or to secure the love of an indifferent fancy, although today this would be viewed as 'black' magic if the spell were against the natural inclinations of the targeted person. This fragment is a translation from *The Religion of Ancient Rome* by Cyril Bailey

May Vettia, daughter of Optata, do whatever I desire, that by your aid for love of me she may not sleep or be able to take food or nourishment. I chain Vettia's sense, wit, understanding, mind and will that she may love me, Felix, son of Fructa, from this day, that she may forget father and mother and all her kith and kin and other friends and for love of me may have me, Felix, only in her mind.

Rather drastic as a love spell but it could be adapted to bind a lover with a fine gold chain to act as a 'binding'.

11. *The Magus*

There are binding spells that have a more sinister reputation, such as the example given in Francis Barrett's 1801 grimoire, *The Magus*, where he lists some of the powers of binding magic:

... the binding of ships, so that no wind, though ever so strong, shall be able to carry them out of the harbour ... the binding of the ground, so that nothing will bring forth fruit ...

On first impression this binding spell could seem more like a curse, but the object behind it is probably only a temporary constraint, to be lifted when the binding has fulfilled its purpose – i.e delaying a competitor.

12. The Roman Binding

Although cited in *Phases in the Religion of Ancient Rome* as a curse, the following is more appropriately 'an old magic ceremony intended to close the mouths of backbiting enemies'. This is a typical instance of a magic rite [binding] with hostile intent taken from Ovid's account in *Fasti*:

With three fingers [the witch] *puts three lumps of incense beneath the threshold* [always a spirit-haunted spot], *where the tiny mouse has made herself a secret path. Then she binds enchanted threads on to the dark magic wheel, and twists and turns seven black beans* [which have always chthonic associations in Roman ritual] *in her mouth. Then she roasts in the fire the head of a spat which she has plastered up with pitch, pierced with a bronze needle* [bronze has magic associations], *and sewn up; she pours in also drops of wine, all the wine that is left she or her companions drink, she more than they; as she departs she says 'We have bound the tongues of foes and the mouths of enemies,' and so she goes tipsy away.*

Cyril Bailey writes that 'here we have a rite, many of whose details are merely intended to create a general atmosphere of magic' – the central and effective parts of the ceremony are the plastering and sewing of the fish's mouth, in a clear act of imitative or homeopathic magic.

13. Simple Bindings

For simple bindings the following chants can be repeated over and over as the cord is wrapped around an image or representation of the person you wish to 'bind'. These are used as temporary restraining measures and as soon as the binding is released, the spell will be nullified. Use either a photograph, or hair, nail parings, etc., wrapped in a piece of clean white paper and roll into a cylinder ready to tie with black twine as you keep up the repetitive chant …

The first is to prevent someone from making a mistake, or acting rashly, and should only have one wrap of the twine before knotting:

Once around, securely bound,
Now is the time for cooling down.

The second is to stop a wagging tongue, gossip or slander, and the cord should be wound around the photograph/paper seven times before knotting:

Suffer thy legs, but not thy tongue to walk;
God, the most wise, is sparing of His talk.

The third is to reveal the perpetrator of some misdeed, i.e. theft, malicious damage, or similar. Here the cord should be wound 13 times before knotting:

When once the sin has fully acted been,
Then is the horror of the trespass seen.

When undoing a binding, *all* the ingredients of the spell must be destroyed, including the paper and twine; burn to ash and then scatter to the four winds. In the case of the last binding, you may wish to retain the ingredients in case some act of retribution is required. In which case, place the rolled photograph/paper inside a glass jar and seal until you have cause to use it.

14. A Truth Spell

The magical community, like any other, is often economical with the truth, and there may be times when we require the truth to be brought into the open. Sometimes people may withhold the truth for protective reasons, in which case you must be sure that you want to hear what is being kept from you. On other occasions you may demand the truth to clear your name or reputation. 'Truth hurts' goes the old saying, so be sure you want to hear it before casting the spell.

To work successfully, the spell requires the creation of an Astral Candle in order to formulate our own subliminal messaging out on the astral levels. To do this you will need the following:

1 purple candle
1 offertory candle in the colour of the sun sign of the one
    withholding the truth
(or white if it is unknown).
Five Senses Oil
Compelling Oil
A needle to mark the candle

This working should be carried out on a Thursday at the hour of Jupiter, the planetary representation for legality (i.e. truth, honesty and justice), and during the phase of the waxing moon. Carve the name of the person you wish to tell the truth on the offertory candle, and anoint it with Five Senses Oil. Anoint the purple candle with the compelling oil. Set the two candles a few inches apart and focus your intent on the outcome you desire.

Focus on the purple candle and say: *'Here is the truth which must be told.'*

Focus on the offertory candle and say: *'Here is* [insert name].*'*

Begin moving the candles closer together until they are touching, and say:

A spell of truth I cast on thee,
Deceit and all confusion flee,
Speak now to her/him,
S/he who I name, [Name]
and she'll do the same.
With clear light I now see,
The truth is clear,
So mote it be.

Take a moment to clarify your intent. Charge the candles again as they burn, adding as you do so:

In no way will this spell reverse

Or place upon me any curse.
Let it be done
In a way that harms none
So mote it be.

Let the candles burn down all the way, standing them in a safe place.

WARNING

Many of the ingredients mentioned in these spells are traditional, i.e. Dove's Blood Ink (a traditional ink for writing spells) or Four Thieves Vinegar (a traditional concoction of vinegar and herbs) and any experienced magical practitioner will be familiar with them. If you have no knowledge, experience or understanding of the materials required, then it would be foolhardy to attempt to use any of the spells. Cursing, hexing, bottling and binding are not for the inexperienced or idly curious – so don't meddle with what you cannot control!

Returning the Hex

Having ascertained that your 'enemy' is genuine, you must decide how you wish to repulse their advances. The form of your retaliation will be decided by your own personality and sense of morality – it is an extension of your own inner mind. There are no hard and fast rules, but do bear in mind that a half-hearted response is just as bad as going over the top. In either case you will have misjudged or misread the situation; alerted your enemy to the fact that you're on to them; and given them the opportunity to change tack. Take a look at your options:

- Double up on personal protection and take defensive measures rather than taking the war into the enemy's camp;
- If you are not 100% sure of the source, channel the returning curse through your personal guardian/deity with the proviso that it should be 'returned from whence it came';
- If you *are* 100% sure of the source and you wish to pay back in kind, then the method, strength and outcome should be magnified three, five, ten or a hundred fold;
- If anger or ego is clouding your judgement, delay the return for 24 hours and reflect.

It is important not to be led astray by ego or paranoia because whatever anyone tells you, it is impossible to recall a curse once it's been sent – which is why you need to be 100% sure of the source before retaliating. What you don't want is to become embroiled in an astral equivalent of *Gunfight at the OK Corral* with magical six-guns blazing – it is tiring, time-consuming and generates nothing but negative energy on both sides.

Bob Clay-Egerton's advice under such circumstances was: 'There is nothing wrong with turning the other cheek, or with forgiving an offence. But there is nothing wrong either with taking protective measures against further slaps. If this is done, then you are perhaps doing a good deed by demonstrating to the attacker that, although you, yourself are not attacking, you are guarding yourself in such a way that their attacks are turned against themselves and that they are, in effect attacking, not you, but themselves. Beware then, not only of excess pride but also of excess humility. Both can be damaging.'

One of the most popular methods of deflecting a curse is to hang an empowered witch-ball in the main entrance hall of your home. The first written record of this method dates back to 1690 where a large glass ball, brightly painted to give a reflective surface to deflect any negative energies coming from any direction and returning them to the sender. A more modern application is the use of a mirrored ball that 'confuses' the energies with its broken or distorted patterns. The curse cannot connect and, having nowhere else to go, goes winging back to the sender, gathering momentum in the process.

Specifically vervain and dill were mentioned in the poem, *Nymphidia*, by Michael Drayton (c1627) – as a protective spell against curses. Accompany the installation of the ball with the sprinkling of those herbs cited in the 17th-century rhyme:

Trefoil, vervain, John's wort, dill
That hindereth witches of the Will.

In *Defences Against the Witches' Craft*, John Canard writes that he is a 'great believer in returning the energy a person puts out to them. If they are sending you negative energy, reflect it to them and let them have a taste of their own medicine. The best way to ensure that somebody does not make the same mistake of directing negativity at you is to switch the tables so they receive what they were trying to give.'

So Mote It Be!

Moon Books invites you to begin or deepen your encounter with
Paganism, in all its rich, creative, flourishing forms.